The Embodiment of Disobedience

The Embodiment of Disobedience

Fat Black Women's Unruly Political Bodies

Andrea Elizabeth Shaw

LEXINGTON BOOKS

A division of
ROWMAN & LITTLEFIELD PUBLISHERS, INC.
Lanham • Boulder • New York • Toronto • Oxford

LEXINGTON BOOKS

A division of Rowman & Littlefield Publishers, Inc.
A wholly owned subsidiary of The Rowman & Littlefield Publishing Group, Inc.
4501 Forbes Boulevard, Suite 200
Lanham, MD 20706

PO Box 317
Oxford
OX2 9RU, UK

British Library Cataloguing in Publication Information Available

Library of Congress Cataloging-in-Publication Data

Shaw, Andrea Elizabeth, 1965–
The embodiment of disobedience : fat black women's unruly political bodies / Andrea Elizabeth Shaw.
p. cm.
Includes index.
ISBN-13: 978-0-7391-1486-5 (cloth : alk. paper)
ISBN-10: 0-7391-1486-7 (cloth : alk. paper)
ISBN-13: 978-0-7391-1487-2 (pbk. : alk. paper)
ISBN-10: 0-7391-1487-5 (pbk. : alk. paper)
1. African American women. 2. Women, Black. 3. African diaspora. 4. Body image—Cross-cultural studies. I. Title.
E185.86.S52 2006
306.4'613—dc22 2006010209

Printed in the United States of America

∞™ The paper used in this publication meets the minimum requirements of American National Standard for Information Sciences—Permanence of Paper for Printed Library Materials, ANSI/NISO Z39.48–1992.

For my mother
Kathleen "Iris" Shaw

For the memory of my father
Burchel Reginald Shaw

Contents

Acknowledgments

First thanks go to my faculty advisor and dissertation chair, Sandra Pouchet Paquet, in the Department of English at the University of Miami. Sandra embraced me and my project in every way. She has been relentless in her support of her students and of Caribbean Literary Studies—an organization that has been the centerpiece of my academic life and the life of many other scholars at U.M.

I would also like to thank the members of my committee, Lindsey Tucker and Frank Stringfellow, who are engaging scholars and teachers. Both Lindsey and Frank have approached my work with great interest and insight, and they have pushed me to refine my ideas and produce a thoughtful project. I am thankful for the benefit of their expertise as well as their ongoing encouragement. I thank Leslie Bow, who was one of the original members of my committee and who agreed to sign on as my outside reader when she left the university. Leslie's suggestions and support have been especially useful at those challenging intellectual junctures. Special thanks to Adele Newson-Horst, who guided me through my M.A. program at Florida International University. It is because of Adele's belief in me and her encouragement that I am able to write these words today.

To my colleagues, in the order they entered the picture: Patricia Saunders, Kezia Page, Kathryn Morris, Kim Dismont Robinson, Joanna Johnson, Maria McGarrity, Javier Reyes and Prudence Layne. Special thanks to Prudence, who was a constant source of support, insight and encouragement, especially as this project came to a close. Over the years these colleagues have always stood ready to offer their advice and assistance; their presence in my life has been priceless.

To my supportive husband Dean Nevins, thank you for believing in me and for taking a sincere interest in my literary pursuits. You have helped me arrive at the end still in one piece. My spectacular children Dean Jr. and Iris, I thank you for being the most engaging and interesting set of children on the planet.

To my brother Paul, whose stellar academic accomplishments and dedication to excellence have helped light the way for me.

Finally, my deepest thanks and appreciation are to my mother, Iris, and my father, Burchel, who have given me a lifetime of support and love that made this book possible and who have dreamed for me what they could not dream for themselves.

Introduction

Fatness and Blackness

A Compelling Coincidence of Erasure

In the United States, fatness and blackness have come to share a remarkably similar and complex relationship with the female body: both characteristics require degrees of erasure in order to render women viable entities by Western aesthetic standards.[1] Beauty pageants attest to this erasure: the more a contestant's body conforms to the cultural ideal of slenderness and the better a contestant can "perform" whiteness both physiologically and behaviorally, the more improved her chances at success. While the images of women dispersed through the various media indirectly recommend whiteness as a necessary component of superior beauty in a racialized cultural environment, slenderness is far less tactfully encouraged. Diet-related products abound on store shelves, in advertisements, and even in virtual space, where pop-up ads entice Internet surfers to drop ten pounds in anywhere from a day to a month. This cultural compulsion to eradicate fat has also manifested as a staple feature of women's magazine articles on how to "banish flab forever" or "tuck your tummy" without surgery. Most recently American health initiatives to "fight obesity" have joined ranks with the surfeit of other cultural expressions that situate fatness as undesirable.

Despite the West's privileging of slenderness, evident in cultural displays such as the Miss America contest, the African Diaspora has historically displayed a resistance to the Western European and North American indulgence in "fat anxiety." This resistance features a clear opposition to the notion that slenderness and health are equivalent. Although signs of this resistance are evident elsewhere in Western culture and civilization, such as lesbian communities and anti-fat discrimination groups, this study surveys the ways in which the African Diaspora has rejected the West's efforts to impose imperatives of slenderness and to mass-market fat anxiety. It also explores the origins and contradictions of this phenomenon, especially the cultural deviations in beauty criteria and the related social and cultural practices. Anchored in literary and cultural readings of the fat black woman's body in the African Diaspora, this book includes discussions of a range of cultural icons such as rap diva Missy Elliott; Carlene, the Caribbean dancehall queen; rhythm and blues songstress Aretha Franklin, and talk-show host Oprah Winfrey. Among the several texts discussed are Alice Randall's *The Wind Done Gone*, Tsitsi Dangarembga's *Nervous Conditions*, Audre Lorde's *Zami: A New Spelling of My Name*, Grace Nichols' *The Fat Black Woman's Poems*, and Derek Walcott's epic *Omeros*.[2] The West has required the ideological erasure of both blackness and fatness as a means of gaining aesthetic acceptability, and these cultural and literary representations of the fat black woman suggest that her body primarily functions as a site of resistance to both gendered and racialized oppression because that body has been the historic locus for assaults against black womanhood.

These requirements for the effacement of blackness are evident in the history of Western beauty contests, and these are an appropriate point of departure from which to investigate the status of black women in contemporary Western beauty culture. One of the earliest beauty pageants held in the United States, and the precursor of the Miss America contest, was the Miss United States contest that was held in Delaware at Rehoboth Beach in 1880.[3] This "bathing" beauty contest was designed as a publicity tool to attract tourism to the resort area and its stipulations for entry into the contest represent an early incantation of the myths of ideal womanhood we hear around us today.[4] Married women were not permitted in the contest, a restriction that valorized virginity and echoed support for the constraint of women's sexual freedom.[5] Additionally, entrants could not be older than twenty-five, had to weigh no more than one hundred and thirty pounds and be at least five feet four inches tall (the requirement of whiteness was apparently so rudimentary that it did not even merit mention by the pageant organizers).[6]

The prize for this first contest was quite appropriately a bridal trousseau, signaling patriarchal reward and recognition for those who best conform to the beauty culture.[7] Additionally, the specificity of the contest's guidelines offered the patriarchy a very precise means of implementing the beauty myth since the pageant would produce a living embodiment of the culture's beauty ideal. Nebulous definitions of beauty began to acquire a distinct form, and with the twentieth century's subsequent growth in technology, pageant images representing these standards could be widely disseminated through the print media and television, thereby firmly asserting white womanhood as the culture's ideal.

Black women were not permitted to participate in the Miss America contest until 1970, on the heels of the Civil Rights Movement, and the first African American Miss America was not crowned until 1984 when Vanessa Williams won the contest.[8] Since then there have been other black winners, and each September the American public sees entrants of diverse ethnic backgrounds sashay across the stage, seemingly indicating that the contest's racist history has been revoked. But has American beauty culture really embraced blackness as a viable feature?

The unwritten contest requisites regarding behavior and appearance demonstrate that the answer is "No," and that the contestants' physiological blackness must be ideologically effaced to render them as acceptable players in the beauty game. In some cases like Williams', her genetic heritage initiates the effacement process. As a biracial woman, her light skin and green eyes immediately denote a "reduction" in her blackness. And in the years since Williams' victory, subsequent black contestants and winners, even those who are darker skinned than Williams, all bear similarly European features such as high cheekbones, straight noses, relatively thin lips, and of course, slender bodies. Additionally, black contestants generally style their hair in a distinctively European manner: flowing shoulder-length tresses or neatly secured buns.

The racial identity of black contestants is further obscured by other behavioral requirements of the contest. During the interview segment, black entrants must further erase any signs of race through their oral delivery. This spoken performance of whiteness must take place on two levels: first, through the black contestants' ability to speak standardized English, and second, through their ability to avoid any speech inflections that would identify them as black (although regional accents that manifest in both black and white entrants seem to be acceptable).[9]

Racial erasure is further encouraged in the talent competition where the participants must display an allegiance to the white middle class. Sarah Banet-Weiser calls this an alliance with "middlebrow" culture, which she defines as that cultural space that is "[n]ot a part of the genteel elite, nor of an unrefined mass, . . . [but] about the acquisition of culture and the educating of oneself in social taste and cultural authority" (108). The term "acquisition" is a crucial nexus in the creation of a non-racialized black identity for contestants, and perhaps more importantly for black women across the U.S.A., and it embodies the ultimate pageant aim and the patriarchal imperative behind it with regard to race—its consumption and absorption by whiteness. Showing black women that admittance into the mainstream beauty culture is achievable by the shedding of their racial identity creates space for racism to justify itself since people of color can simply move out of their problematic racial category: if you can become "white," why concern yourself with perceived racial bias and antagonism?

One pageant handbook written by Genie Sayles and quoted by Sarah Banet-Weiser emphasizes choice as an important component for success in the talent competition, and exercising choice is also ultimately crucial for negotiating a white-dominated multiracial society:

> There is no excuse for anything less than perfection in talent competition. Talent is the one competition you have more control over than any other. You may not have chosen your body structure or your facial features. You may not have been asked a single question in interview that you studied months for. You may not be able to afford a velvet and gold lamé dress for evening gown. But you—You choose your talent! . . . You choose the image you will convey . . . you choose how flawlessly you will perform your talent. You CHOOSE that. (Sayles, qtd. in Banet-Weiser 111)

The pageant's "talent" competition then becomes a euphemism for honing survival skills to overcome racial limitations.

Performing acts that Sayles describes as "folk talent" can cost contestants in the long run, whereas performative ventures that display an effort to replicate elitist culture, even if poorly performed, will probably net the contestant a more lucrative score.[10] By performing acts that reflect an exposure to white, middle-class cultural values, black participants lessen the impact of their black bodies, and efforts to reinscribe their blackness are discouraged by pageant officials. When one black contestant debated between singing Whitney Houston's "I'm Going to Run to You" and Liza Minnelli's "Cabaret," the pageant organizers suggested the Minnelli song.[11] But in a conversation later that evening, the contestant admitted that she liked the Houston song and feared that the judges would think, "She's just another black girl doing Whitney Houston."[12] Houston's popularity as a black performer superimposed on the black body of the contestant would disrupt the pageant's myth of acquired whiteness, making the Houston song a less favorable choice.

No doubt this oppressive beauty culture that manifests in national contests throughout the African Diaspora has recently been aided by the advent of satellite technology that facilitates the dissemination of American culture around the world, reinforcing racist beauty ideology already in existence. The Miss America contest and similar national contests are then critical sites for imposing neocolonial beauty imperatives upon black women, and the construction of a middlebrow beauty contest culture that encourages and even requires the erasure of blackness is not unique to America and exists across the Diaspora.

In Jamaica the recognition of the national Miss Jamaica pageant as an effort to deny and diminish the country's overwhelming African heritage was clear to the audience at the 1986 Miss Jamaica finals, and the announcement of the winner elicited an angry and vociferous response. When

Lisa Mahfood, a light-skinned, straight-haired Jamaican of Middle Eastern ancestry, was crowned Miss Jamaica, the crowd erupted in shouts and jeers and hurled debris on the stage.[13] This impassioned reaction can be better understood in the historical context of Jamaica's beauty pageants. Starting in the forties, the contests were open exclusively to white Creole girls, but eventually the ideological disparity between the ethnicity of the contestants and the racial composition of the Jamaican population drew varying efforts to placate an increasingly disenchanted public.[14] Among various efforts to assuage the pageant's black Jamaican audience was the development of the "Ten Types; One People" contest in 1955.[15] This ludicrous effort subdivided the Miss Jamaica pageant into 10 different racially specific contests. Names like "Miss Ebony" (for dark-skinned women), "Miss Apple Blossom" (for white Creoles), and "Miss Allspice" (for women of East Indian parentage) euphemistically denoted the racial groups for whom those contests were intended.[16] Despite this comedic and unsuccessful attempt at inclusion, thirty years later Lisa Mahfood was crowned Miss Jamaica, reinvigorating the resentment that spawned the "Ten Types" competition.

Similar considerations over the representational politics of beauty contests have brewed in the Kingdom of Swaziland over the choice of a young colored woman as Miss Swaziland in 1991. During her reign as queen, photographs of Jackie Bennett were published in a local newspaper spread showing her in Western-style dress wearing sunglasses and a miniskirt, indicating her entrance into Western beauty culture and suggesting that as a requirement traditional Swazi dress must either be eliminated or at times exchanged with Western fashion.[17] While the article on Bennett reports no public outcry over her crowning, her images in the newspapers raise questions about the ways in which physiological black erasure creates greater access to alternate, nontraditional means of self-representation. Moreover, could her decision to include a wardrobe of Western fashion be a necessary marker of eligibility for entry into Westernized Swazi beauty culture?

The disruptive potential of national pageants and their function as a site for negotiating national concerns reveal the extensive political dimensions of a country's beauty culture and the complex roots from which that culture has evolved. Unlike the choice of national bird or national dish, the country's beauty queen represents the gendered and racialized identity that a nation decides to assume. As a result, dissatisfaction with the choice of a beauty ambassador often leads to ideological embattlement in preparation for an incensed cultural debate over who deserves the nation's aesthetic crown, and ultimately over the nation's chosen identity. The beauty queen's body becomes a speculum of the political climate with regard to race and gender, and competing bodies that become entangled in beauty politics volley not only for the appropriation of "beautiful," but as bodily representations of the national identity.

Given the relatively recent admission of black women such as Naomi Campbell and Tyra Banks into the world of fashion and beauty, some may argue that whiteness is no longer the zenith of Western beauty and femininity. However, national pageants that regulate each nation's conceptualization of the feminine ideal seem to compel black erasure on some level, and when a black woman wins a national competition, the insidious racial agenda at work is often betrayed by the choice of a near-white or lightly complexioned black woman as an image of ultimate beauty (as accommodated by a black body). These beauty contests then become an inverted form of minstrelsy, requiring the hopeful participants to perform in "white face." However, the identity choice represented by these light-skinned women is situated in an inaccessible mythological realm for most black women. And those who hurl oranges onto the Miss Jamaica stage, or write angry letters to Vanessa Williams disparaging her light-colored eyes, recognize the futility of embarking on a quest to share in the identity she represents.[18] Williams' body and that of all black beauty queens in Western culture must conform to pageant guidelines that promote a foregrounding of whiteness despite a black genetic heritage. This requirement is for a "phantasmatic" identity that can never be realized, since all efforts towards erasing blackness create a spectral shadow that even further embeds that blackness in place by the obviousness of its absence, and through acts of resistance toward that erasure.[19]

African Diaspora cultures have historically displayed a resistance to the idealization of slenderness evident in Westernized beauty contests, and the value of a robust female body among certain African tribes is underscored by an 1852 picture taken in the Sudan and titled "A Nubian Warrior with His Wife, a Local Beauty Prized for Her Weight" (Willis and Williams 13).[20] This picture features a young couple; the man is tall and slender, dressed in what appears to be some sort of ceremonial garb, and his wife stands beside him, a very large woman, fully clothed as a mark of her social position. The picture clearly reflects an alternative aesthetic paradigm to the current North American beauty culture, which would find little room to aesthetically value an overweight, dark-skinned woman, let alone to consider her a "local beauty," befitting of marriage to a male of outstanding social status.[21]

The high esteem placed on an ample female physique is further evident among several African tribes through the cultural phenomenon of "fatting houses." A prominent feature in West Africa, fatting houses are designed to prepare young women for matrimony. Teenaged girls are sent to the fatting house in batches, and during their tenure they are sequestered from public view, fed substantial portions of food, and restricted in their physical movement to maximize their weight-gaining potential.[22] These efforts are aimed at maximizing the girls' weight to increase their attractiveness and consequently their marriage opportunities. Furthermore, fatting houses are an important site of cultural ingestion, and they contribute to the development of young tribeswomen beyond enhancing their aesthetic appeal:

> It used to be thought that the girls just went into the fatting-house to get fat and idle away their time. This is nonsense. Actually, during the time of their seclusion they were given serious instruction in dancing, comb-making, care of children, embroidery, and many other things. (Madame Grace Davis qtd. in Thompson 230)[23]

These fatting houses can be read, then, as socio-cultural storehouses that impart tradition and endurance skills to prepare these girls for adulthood. Hence, the physical fat that they take away with them on their bodies is a symbol of the cultural immersion that fatting houses represent and locate the girls in a specific aesthetic realm with Afrocentric roots. Because of this value attached to the copious woman's body, depictions of the gaunt female body in African literature sometimes function as a trope for desexualization. Flora Veit-Wild explains:

> While the traditional positive image of the African woman was one of corpulence (there were special "fattening rooms" for young girls before marriage), modern literature presents prominent examples of women struggling —or threatening men—with the destruction of their own bodies. (128)[24]

The image of the slender body is also represented in Tsitsi Dangarembga's *Nervous Conditions*, in which anorexia is presented as the destabilizing result of colonialization.[25]

In other parts of the black Diaspora, the slim body also suggests dearth, and fatness occupies a space where it metaphorically signifies the abundance associated with fatting houses. An African American woman recalls her experiences growing up fat, and she notes that her self-perception shifted depending on where she lived. While working in a predominantly black town in rural Mississippi, she was comfortable with her size because of the cultural environment:

> I have been overweight for most of my life, but its significance has waxed and waned depending on the environment in which I lived. Those good people in Pinola, Mississippi loved me as I loved them. They thought I was beautiful. "You's a good lookin' gal. Healthy. Got flesh. Chile, you sho' is fine." (Bass 224)[26]

Pinola can be read as an incubation site for the African aesthetic values responsible for the development of fatting houses; for the black residents of this community, fatness was desirable. In Caribbean culture there is a similar appreciation of the black woman's body, and this coalesces in the myth of Jamaican folk hero Grandy Nanny, who could supposedly stop the bullets from the white soldiers with her buttocks.[27] This myth positions Nanny's fatness—represented by her buttocks—as not only appreciable but as a form of (neo)colonial resistance.

Regardless of size, one uniting characteristic in the iconography of black women is that they inhabit a space largely defined by its sexuality. In her essay "Selling Hot Pussy: Representations of Black Female Sexuality in the Cultural Marketplace," bell hooks discusses the stage persona of various black female celebrities, and she suggests that their sexuality has been a dominant constituent of their public profile.[28] But what hooks does not address is the stage persona of fat black women and the ways in which their size intersects with popular notions of black female sexuality. These would include women like Ma Rainey and Bessie Smith—blues divas of the 1920s, rhythm and blues singers Aretha Franklin, Jill Scott and Angie Stone, or rappers Queen Latifah and Missy Elliott—all women who have risen to fame or sustained their fame with fat physiques. These singers incorporate their bodies into their sexual identity, and for the most part their bodies are dressed in ways that mark them as sexually viable and attractive. Despite more dominant oppositional ideals, these women resist both slenderness and whiteness as the exclusive realms of beauty. The conspicuous absence of a proportionate number of white counterparts to these large black performers suggests that size and white female sexuality intersect in different ways in the cultural marketplace. Fatness as the embodiment of sexuality is acceptable only when strategically placed on the bodies of white women; however, black women's status as "other" allows their fat and subsequently hypersexualized image to be more acceptable. Thus large white female singers such as Wynonna Judd and Carnie Wilson before she lost weight dress their bodies attractively, but not in an overtly sexual manner.

Black women's bodies and their sexuality are important symbols in African diasporic literature because these bodies are often the site of literal and metaphorical racist and sexist assaults. Furthermore, their bodies sometimes function metonymically as the representational site of political conflict. The examples abound; they range from the visage of Mavis's mutilated breast that closes Orlando Patterson's *Children of Sisyphus,* to the cherry tree pattern of scar tissue "growing" on Sethe's back in Toni Morrison's *Beloved*.[29] Regarding Caribbean women's writing, Denise deCaires Narain suggests the following:

> The body has become increasingly important as the site of a series of contested inscriptions and readings. In the context of feminist criticisms woman's body has been perceived as one of the most dramatic—and contradictory—sites of the struggle against patriarchy. (98)[30]

On the other hand, Anne-Marie Gronhovd argues that "The performance that takes place in the writing and the reading of the woman's body traced by the mind of that same woman creates her identity as she invents herself," recognizing the transformative potential inherent in engaging the body from a creative perspective (102).[31]

Despite all the scholarly attention given to the female body, there is a paucity of work that explores the fat black woman's body and how its literary and cultural presence may differ from or reinforce certain theories regarding female physicality. This project pursues compelling intersections between cultural perceptions of fatness and blackness on the site of the female body, and more specifically, this study is concerned with the literary and cultural political implications of existing within this doubly marginalized space. This project also explores how the full-figured body fits into the colonial landscape. In other words, the primary aim of this project is to develop a theoretical framework that may be used to "read" the fat black woman's literary and cultural body.

Throughout the African Diaspora the fat black woman's body operates as a polyvalent retaliatory agent that responds to the impact of colonization. Her body-size is configured to share a proportionate relationship to her textual function regarding the extent of the colonial rupture she addresses—the larger her body the more damaging the effects of colonization to which she responds. Her fat, which codes her as a repository of latent energy, symbolizes the mediating and healing resources often associated with the literary bodies of large black women. But her function is not necessarily docile and overtly reparatory; she may address concerns in the text through her unruliness and rebellion that are implicit in her size. Her resistance to authoritative cultural requirements does not necessarily signal that she is not capable of complying; her fat may indicate an *unwillingness* to comply, or an *indifference* to those norms. Accordingly, her disruptive and unruly behavior becomes her way of effecting control and order within the confines of the circumstances she encounters. Her size further illustrates her chosen disobedience since its corpulence may also be read as sufficiency and therefore a lack of desire to ingest the alien ideologies that have already rendered her beyond the periphery of the dominant culture.

The fat black woman's body poses a dual challenge to the colonially inspired dominant aesthetic norms that are instituted as a political mechanism for control; these norms symbolize the hegemonic force from which they arise. Her fat black body resists both imperatives of whiteness and slenderness as an ideal state of embodiment. Her large size also insists that her presence be acknowledged since a pervasive effect of colonization has been the effacement of a black female presence through the dismissal of conflicts and concerns attendant to the displacement experienced by women of African descent. The fat black woman's hyper-embodiment is also a metaphorical form of resistance to her negation from both white and/or male-authored bodies of literature as well as to hegemonic aesthetic imperatives.

The negation and erasure of both size and race to which this project attends is recapitulated by the responses to one of the oldest works of art: the Venus of Willendorf—a limestone statue discovered in Austria in 1908 that features a full-bodied woman.[32] The four and a half inch statue features a naked, fat woman with large breasts, a clearly defined pubic area, and raised circular bands around her head, and it dates to around 24,000–22,000 BCE during the Palaeolithic Age.[33] Is she some sort of Stone Age goddess—an exaggerated female form that represents a cultural wish for fertility or abundance? Is she the artist's wife? Is she the artist? Or could this fat woman—the oldest known representation of the human body—with pendulous breasts and large thighs have been that age's icon of beauty?[34]

The Venus of Willendorf's identity is further obscured if we consider race. She was carved during the Aurignacian period of the Palaeolithic Age by a prehistoric people known as Grimaldi Man.[35] The Grimaldis were black Homo sapiens migrants from Africa and the first inhabitants of Europe.[36] Other pieces of Aurignacian art produced by the Grimaldis imply that she is racially representative of her creators since they "faithfully reproduced the physical type of the race, not only that of the typical African woman, but also that of the typical African man" (Diop 45). Furthermore, her hairstyle closely resembles cornrows, the currently popular hair fashion among black women, suggesting that the woman/women after whom she was modeled were of African origin. So, in our Western society where women are subjected to the "tyranny of slenderness,"[37] and drug stores are filled with products to reduce bodily manifestations of blackness, what does it mean for this celebrated, ancient work of art to be the naked body of a fat black woman? It seems to mean the same as it does for those whose real, live bodies are similarly black, fat and female: banishment to the periphery of Western beauty consciousness.

This marginalization process for the Venus of Willendorf began when she was dubbed with the sobriquet "Venus" like several of the other corpulent female stone-age sculptures unearthed in the 1800s.[38] The term Venus evokes images of the Roman goddess of love and beauty or her Greek counterpart Aphrodite, usually depicted as nude, erotic and white. Naming this twenty-four thousand year old statue "Venus" effects the kind of parodic control created when slave-masters named their slaves after royalty. The obviousness of the disjunction between the *name* and the *named* creates such an ironic contrast that the disparaged group is more firmly embedded in the culture's consciousness as existing in marginalized territory that cannot readily be absorbed into the space the name implies. The use of this naming convention effectively replicates the ways in which white patriarchal power utilizes beauty as a virulent means of female circumscription that subordinates other signifying values to its control—such as being the earliest known artistic creation.

Reinforcing these white patriarchal values, one anthropologist emphatically insists that it is preposterous to think that the Venus of Willendorf could *ever* have represented *any* culture's image of beauty: "these archetypal figures cannot be attributed to the 'sexual taste' of the male. There is no doubt that the relationship between 'taste' and the figure is just the opposite and far more complex" (Neumann 97).[39] This resistance to embracing the Venus of Willendorf's fat body as attractive may initially appear unnecessary to the current patriarchal beauty initiative. After all, how can a stone-age carving upset the firmly rooted power of the Western, male gaze? But it is significant because the reification of Western beauty consciousness depends upon its establishment as an uninterrupted, unchallenged standard of measurement that is never subject to reconsideration or reinterpretation.

It is not only the Venus of Willendorf's corpulence that permanently situates her in a ghost-land of offensive bodies. It is also her racial identity. While her significance as the oldest work of art cannot be ignored, her race can be. As a result, through a sort of racial exorcism her offending blackness has been isolated and detached, which renders her body more agreeable to the white power-structure. And so in several texts that discuss the Venus of Willendorf, there is no reference to the group of people thought to be her creator and, as a result, no discussion of her race.[40] Physiological traits like her hairstyle and hair texture that help identify her as black are ignored. In one text the suggestion is made that she could be wearing a hat.[41] In another, it is adamantly insisted upon that her steatopygia,[42] common among the African Hottentot tribe, was not related to "any racial characteristics."[43] This effacement of the Venus of Willendorf's race is inscribed by an act of ethnic disinheritance achieved by presenting her in a racial void to prevent her racial identity from piggybacking into the arena of cultural acceptability based upon her cultural significance.

This book explores similar efforts aimed at devaluing blackness as well as the treatment of fatness as yet another marginalized physical identity. The project is arranged in four chapters and each examines different representational aspects relating to the fat black woman's body. The chapters combine both literary and cultural "texts" as a part of the study, and these include novels, poems, stories, film, television shows, and advertisements. Additionally, historical material and autobiographical details are incorporated. This broad range of material grounds the book's argument beyond the literary sphere and draws strong connections between the literary treatment of large black women and their social treatment with regard to historic or popular cultural sentiment. Indeed, while chapters one through three feature a range of printed material, the fourth and final chapter is primarily anchored in cultural readings of biographical research on the careers of several entertainers.

CHAPTER ONE

Chapter one engages the notion of identity and illuminates the role of the fat black woman's body in the process of identity creation. This chapter also interrogates tensions between varying cultural notions of beauty and explores the complex nature of the historical relationship between black and white women. It illustrates how constructions of beauty were used to enforce the hegemonic agenda of the patriarchy and how the Western conceptualization of idealized femininity as exclusively white is an important means of sustaining racialized hierarchies because it is able to concurrently devalue both race and gender.[44] Chapter one also examines how the large black female body affects the formation of black and white identity and argues that the fat black woman's image is an indicator of an "illegitimate" aesthetic embodiment according to Western conventions of beauty. It begins with a discussion of the slave Mammy, one of the most dominant images of black womanhood in the U.S.A., and analyzes how her image has impacted notions of both black and white femininity. Her role in the shaping of ideas related to identity formation is a conflicted one in which she functions as both a behavioral example for white women to emulate and a physiological example for them to avoid. Mammy's life is dedicated to the domestic realm, but simultaneously she is an inverse physiological speculum of idealized womanhood—large, dark, lumbering and yet capable, versus being of a diminutive size, light-skinned, graceful, delicate and dependent. In addition to discussing Mammy's cultural evolution within a North American context, the chapter also discusses her literary production, specifically in Alice Randall's *The Wind Done Gone*. Subsequently, to further explore the relationship between fatness, blackness and female identity, the chapter includes readings of Joan Riley's *Romance* and Tsitsi Dangarembga's *Nervous Conditions*—both novels that explore the impact of race and Western beauty ideal upon black women's self-perception.[45]

CHAPTER TWO

This chapter examines the fat black woman's hypersexualization, which is doubly signified by both her size and her race and constructed as a form

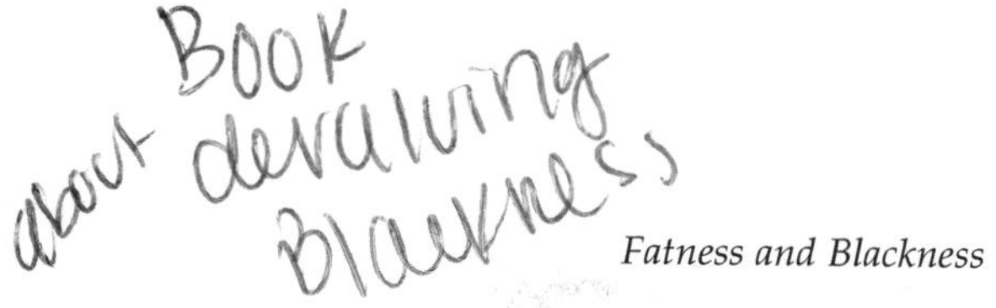

of sexual deviance. The chapter begins with an assessment of the experiences of Saartjie Baartman, the Hottentot Venus—a large black woman taken from South Africa and displayed in Europe during the 1800s. Baartman's oppressive experiences are positioned in tandem with the evolution of black female sexuality in the Western World. Furthermore, the large black woman's sexuality is often invoked as a form of neo-resistance to hegemonic forms of oppression. Chapter two also includes a discussion of the cultural representations of fatness and blackness, referring to television characters such as Miss Piggy from *The Muppets* and Mrs. Parker from *The Parkers.* Additionally, the chapter engages a range of texts that feature highly sexualized fat black women. These texts include Grace Nichols' *The Fat Black Woman's Poems,* Anthony Winkler's *The Duppy* and Audre Lorde's *Zami.*[46]

CHAPTER THREE

The third chapter charts the iconographic link between the bodies of large black women and notions of economic abundance. Again, portions of the chapter's argument are grounded in popular cultural expressions of fat black femininity such as the Caribbean higgler and in the fatting house ritual of Western Africa. The core argument in this chapter is that fatness operates in resistance to some dominant assumptions about blackness—invisibility and the inability to manage and accumulate resources. This hypothesis is further extended using Karl Marx's theory of surplus value to suggest that fatness on the bodies of black women operates as a form of redress for stolen labor. The literary analysis is anchored with a discussion of Derek Walcott's *Omeros,* and to a lesser extent Gloria Naylor's *Mama Day* and Alice Walker's *The Color Purple.*[47]

CHAPTER FOUR

The final chapter engages the performing bodies of large black women, mainly on the North American concert stage, and explores the question of how in a culture where these women are marginalized because of both their size and race, so many of them have managed to achieve phenomenal success in the musical entertainment industry. In response to this curious occurrence the chapter begins by first discussing the evolution of women in the American theater and then by suggesting that the transgressive nature of the performance stage as a site for the production of the spectacular has been particularly accommodating to large black women because both their race and size are transgressive signifiers that efficiently facilitate the creation of the spectacular. Among the performers discussed are blues diva Ma Rainey, rhythm and blues queen Aretha Franklin, and rap star Missy Elliott. There are also discussions of Jamaican dancehall and Trinidadian soca aesthetics within the context of the spectacular.

This project concludes by suggesting that the association of health and happiness with the slender body, in addition to cultural imperatives to control the body to sustain its slenderness, arise from a need to displace anxieties over the West's ever-increasing and uncontrollable consumption of material goods, and reasserts the main idea that underscores this study: the fat black woman's body primarily functions in a resistive and transgressive mode because her body has been the site of historic efforts to devalue black womanhood.

NOTES

1. Several of my terminologies multitask and may refer to both a geographic site as well as ideologies related to the territorial locale. One such example is my use of the terms "Western" or the "West." In some instances I use these terms to mean the physical locales generally identified as the West: Western Europe and North America. However, on other occasions I refer to the cultural values that have arisen from Western civilization—that system of cultural and political ideals with its roots in ancient Greece and ancient Rome and that has informed the dominant aesthetic values of North American and European societies.

2. Alice Randall, *The Wind Done Gone* (Boston: Houghton Mifflin Company, 2001); Tsitsi Dangarembga, *Nervous Conditions* (Seattle: Seal Press, 1989); Grace Nichols, *The Fat Black Woman's Poems* (London: Virago Press, 1984); Audre Lorde, *Zami: A New Spelling of My Name* (Freedom, Calif.: The Crossing Press, 1982); Derek Walcott, *Omeros* (New York: Farrar, Straus and Giroux, 1990).

3. Frank Deford, *There She Is: The Life and Times of Miss America* (New York: Penguin Books, 1971), 108.

4. A. R. Riverol, *Live From Atlantic City* (Bowling Green, Ohio: Bowling Green State University Popular Press, 1992), 9.

5. Riverol, *Live From Atlantic City*, 10.

6. Riverol, *Live From Atlantic City*, 10.

7. Riverol, *Live From Atlantic City*, 9.

8. Sarah Banet-Weiser, *The Most Beautiful Girl in the World* (Berkeley: University of California Press, 1999), 127.

9. Banet-Weiser explains that beauty contestants cite the interview portion of the competition as quite valuable since it helps them to develop public-speaking skills and to cultivate a "rehearsed spontaneity" (94).

10. Banet-Weiser, *The Most Beautiful Girl in the World*, 111.

11. Banet-Weiser, *The Most Beautiful Girl in the World*, 116.

12. Banet-Weiser, *The Most Beautiful Girl in the World*, 116.

13. Natasha Barnes, "Face of the Nation: Race, Nationalisms and Identities in Jamaican Beauty Pageants," *Massachusetts Review* 35, nos. 3–4 (Fall 1994): 471–92. For a further account of events at the contest, see "Missiles Barrage at Beauty Contest," *Daily Gleaner*, September 8, 1986.

14. Barnes, "Face of the Nation," 473.

15. Barnes, "Face of the Nation," 478.

16. Barnes, "Face of the Nation," 478.

17. Carolyn Behrman, "'The Fairest of Them All': Gender, Ethnicity, and a Beauty Pageant in the Kingdom of Swaziland," *Dress and Ethnicity*, ed. Joanne B. Eicher (Oxford: Berg Publishers Limited, 1995), 402.

18. Banet-Weiser, *The Most Beautiful Girl in the World*, 136. See Banet-Weiser's brief discussion of the angry letters Vanessa Williams received from people who were upset about her light complexion and from members of the public who became aware she was dating a white man.

19. Judith Butler, *Bodies That Matter: On the Discursive Limits of "Sex"* (New York: Routledge, 1993), 93–119. See Butler's chapter "Phantasmatic Identification and the Assumption of Sex," where she discusses the construction of sexual identity and the "normalization of (hetero)sexuality" (93).

20. Deborah Willis and Carla Williams, *The Black Female Body: A Photographic History* (Philadelphia: Temple University Press, 2002).

21. While there is the possibility that the photographer applied the title "local beauty" with some cynical undertones, this sarcasm would be more a reflection that his taste conflicted with those of his African subjects than an indication that the woman in the photograph was not really considered beautiful.

22. *Monday's Girls*, directed by Ngozi Onwyrah. Videocassette. California Newsreel, 1994.

23. Robert Farris Thompson, *Flash of the Spirit: African and Afro-American Art and Philosophy* (New York: Vintage Books, 1984).

24. Flora Veit-Weld, "Borderlines of the Body in African Women's Writing," *Borderlands: Negotiating Boundaries in Postcolonial Writing*, ed. Monika Reif-Hulser (Amsterdam: Rodopi, 1999).

25. Heike Harting, "The Profusion of Meanings and the Female Experience of Colonisation: Inscriptions of the Body as a Site of Difference in Tsitsi Dangarembga's *Nervous Conditions* and Margaret Atwood's *The Edible Woman*," *Fusion of Cultures*, eds. Peter Stummer and Christopher Balme (Amsterdam: Rodopi, 1996), 237–46.

26. Margart K. Bass, "On Being a Fat Black Girl in a Fat-Hating Culture," *Recovering the Black Female Body: Self-Representations by African American Women*, eds. Michael Bennett and Vanessa D. Dickerson (New Brunswick, N.J.: Rutgers University Press, 2001), 219–30.

27. Mara Scanlon, "The Divine Body in Grace Nichols's *The Fat Black Woman's Poems*," *World Literature Today: A Quarterly of the University of Oklahoma* 1 (1998 Winter): 59–66.

28. bell hooks, "Selling Hot Pussy: Representations of Black Female Sexuality in the Cultural Marketplace," *Writing on the Body*, eds. Katie Conboy, Nadia Medina and Sarah Stanbury (New York: Columbia University Press, 1997), 113–28.

29. H. Orlando Patterson, *The Children of Sisyphus* (Boston: Houghton Mifflin, 1965); Toni Morrison, *Beloved* (New York: Knopf, 1987).

30. Denise deCaires Narain, "The Body of the Woman in the Text: The Novels of Erna Brodber," *Caribbean Women Writers: Fictions in English*, eds. Mary Condé and Thorunn Lonsdale (New York: St. Martin's Press, 1999), 97–116.

31. Anne-Marie Gronhovd, "Writing the Woman-Subject : Marguerite Duras, from Theory to Fiction," *International Women's Writing: New Landscapes of Identity*, eds. Anne E. Brown and Marjanne Gooze (Westport, Conn.: Greenwood, 1995), 102–11.

32. Christopher L. C. E. Witcombe, "Women in Prehistory: The Venus of Willendorf—Discovery," *Art History Resources on the Web* (1995), Sweet Briar College. Accessed September 18, 2002, <http://witcombe.sbc.edu/willendorfdiscovery.html>.

33. Witcombe, "Women in Prehistory: The Venus of Willendorf—Discovery."

34. Ivan Van Sertima, *Black Women in Antiquity* (New Brunswick, N.J.: Transaction Publishers, 1987), 138.

35. Cheikh Anta Diop, *Civilization or Barbarism: An Authentic Anthropology*, trans. Yaa-Lengi Meema Ngemi (Brooklyn: Lawrence Hill Books), 45.

36. Diop, *Civilization or Barbarism*, 13–15.

37. Kim Chernin, *The Obsession: Reflections on the Tyranny of Slenderness* (New York: Harper and Row, 1981).

38. Witcombe, "Women in Prehistory: The Venus of Willendorf—What's in a Name?"

39. Erich Neumann, *The Great Mother: An Analysis of the Archetype*, Bollingen Series 47 (Princeton: Princeton University Press, 1963).

40. See Witcombe, "Women in Prehistory: The Venus of Willendorf—Discovery"; Neumann, *The Great Mother*, 97; Anne Scott Beller, *Fat and Thin: A Natural History of Obesity* (New York: Farrar, Straus & Giroux, 1978), 70–73; Peter Stepan, ed., *Icons of Europe* (New York: Prestel, 2002), 18.

41. Stepan, *Icons of Europe*, 18.

42. The Merriam-Webster online dictionary defines "steatopygia" as "an excessive development of fat on the buttocks that occurs especially among women of the Hottentots and some black peoples." "Steatopygia," *Merriam-Webster's Online Dictionary*, 2004, University of Miami Ibisweb, accessed July 6, 2004.

43. Neumann, *The Great Mother*, 97.

44. Because of the gender issues raised by my discourse, I use the term "patriarchal" when I want to emphasize the male-female dichotomies inherent in a cultural phenomenon. I use this term in reference to those value systems that privilege maleness, but which quite often are anchored in a larger system that disfavors people of color. As a result, at times the term might seem conflictive in its application, but I see this as no less problematic than the actual subscription of men of color to ideologies which concurrently marginalize them because of their race while privileging them because of their gender. I also refer to a "white power structure," a term which I use when I want to focus attention on the racial aspects of an oppressive political and economic relationship. I perceive this racially inflected power structure as a portion of the same system from which "patriarchal" ideals spring.

45. Joan Riley, *Romance* (London: The Women's Press, 1988); Tsitsi Dangarembga, *Nervous Conditions* (Seattle: Seal Press, 1989).

46. Anthony C. Winkler, *The Duppy* (Kingston, Jamaica: LMH Publishing Ltd., 1997).

47. Gloria Naylor, *Mama Day* (New York: Vintage Contemporaries, 1993); Alice Walker, *The Color Purple* (New York: Pocket Books, 1985).

1

Reshaping Identity

The overwhelming economic and cultural authority of the West, and the success with which it has imposed Eurocentric values on subaltern populations, has had a major impact—both material and social—on the lives of black women throughout the Diaspora. In Western culture, whiteness has come to be the defining zenith of physical attractiveness, and Western conventions of what constitute socially acceptable beauty devalue both race and gender of subaltern populations simultaneously, making fatness and blackness physical attributes that have historically restricted the fat black woman from being considered beautiful relative to Western culture's definitions of beauty. Nevertheless, the large black female body has had a significant role in the formation of both black and white identity throughout the Diaspora because it functions as an opposing identity anchor—an image that affirms "legitimate" identity as different from what that image represents. This chapter's exploration of identity is anchored in readings of Alice Randall's controversial novel, *The Wind Done Gone*, Tsitsi Dangarembga's *Nervous Conditions*, and Joan Riley's *Romance*.

The mythical figure of Mammy is central to the discussion of black female identity and constitutes a phantasmic point of identity—an identity that can never be realized.[1] Patricia Hill Collins defines the Mammy image as follows:

> The first controlling image applied to African American women is that of the mammy—the faithful, obedient domestic servant. Created to justify the economic exploitation of house slaves and sustained to explain black women's

> long-standing restriction to domestic service, the mammy image represents the normative yardstick used to evaluate all Black women's behavior. (71)[2]

Whereas the black beauty queen's physical and cultural heritage must mimic white physiology and behavior, Mammy's blackness is intensified and exaggerated, foregrounding her black physiology as the center of her identity.[3] Despite their disparity, Mammy's image serves the same function as that of the black beauty queen; it mollifies racial anxieties by rendering a physiological black presence acceptable to white-inflected beauty culture. Mammy, in her head rag with grinning teeth and enormous body, is alter ego to lithe, fair-skinned Vanessa Williams.

White patriarchal embrace of Mammy's fictional and commercial image in the United States alternately masks and communicates an effort to locate and elide blackness through exaggeration. The result is a formulated and unrepresentative staging of black womanhood that conforms to a white hegemonic ideal of an acquiescent, subordinate, and nondisruptive version of black femininity. One of Mammy's main functions derives, perhaps predominantly, from her asexuality. The contrariness of her large body, dark skin and non-angular facial features to the ideal image of Western beauty causes Mammy to pose no sexual threat to white women.[4] By deflecting attention from sexually attractive black women resembling Vanessa Williams, the Mammy image mollifies white female fears about white men's interracial liaisons.

The fictional image of the large Mammy, lumbering around the plantation great house, an image reproduced in films such as *Gone With the Wind* (1936), also serves the white patriarchy by helping to more firmly define patriarchal imperatives for white women. As the physical embodiment of features rejected by Western beauty criteria, Mammy becomes a shadow against which white women's beauty may be foregrounded. As a dominant image of the "other," Mammy helps to sustain the rhizomic connections of economic, gendered and racial oppression by defining the opposing physical standards by which white female identity is formed.[5] The mythical Mammy figure historically served dual roles in defining white female identity. Although she provided a physical contrast, the black mammy's identity was anchored in the domestic sphere and was highlighted by her dedication to the smooth operation of the household and the welfare of the children in that household.[6]

Because the maternal qualities of Mammy's image situate her exclusively in the domestic sphere, she also functions as a divisive mechanism that further anchors white control by creating tension between black men and women.[7] In order to provide instant caregiving for her white masters/employers, black female domestic servants, upon whom Mammy is modeled, needed to be in close proximity. As a result, Mammy could develop intimate connections and make use of opportunities created by this proximity that worked both for and against the interests of a beleaguered black community.

In addition to signaling the compromise of black, intraracial relationships, Mammy's large body also represents an overabundance of maternal resources. This characteristic feature of her motherly largesse perhaps functions as an even more lethal and potent form of subjugation than Mammy's asexuality. In the role as a domestic caretaker, she represents the ultimate state of black allegiance to whiteness: the ready availability of nurture despite her own economic oppression effected by those she must serve.[8] Her fatness signals an infinite reserve of maternal dedication, suggesting an *inability* of black women to be oppressed since their supply of strength, love, and other emotional resources can never be depleted. Furthermore, the link between fat and motherhood implies an inclination, if not need, to serve as a caretaker, which in turn implies a sadomasochistic element of desire and fulfillment in black women's experience of economic abuse and marginalization, and mitigates moral responsibility on the part of her abusers.

Despite the post–Civil Rights, postcolonial emphasis on cultural pluralism in the U.S.A. and the West, the "otherness" of black women and black people continues to be a defining characteristic of Western culture.[9] One of the recent trends has been a commercial attempt to capture some element of this otherness for economic exploitation. Asian and African artifacts now abound in department stores, tropical/third-world settings are often used for promotional catalogs, and supermarkets seem to be devoting increasing amounts of shelf space to "ethnic" foods.[10] Mammy has also fallen prey to this commodification of difference in the contemporary reinvention of the atavistic figure of Aunt Jemima.

The Quaker Oats trademark, which originally featured a full-bodied black woman costumed as a plantation servant, sidesteps the historical legacy of slavery by refashioning that history for consumption and enjoyment by both black and white Americans. The modified Mammy shares a mythical genesis like her predecessor and feeds the same capitalist appetite that fueled slavery. Accounts of Aunt Jemima's origins are not well documented, but one version indicates that this ubiquitous trademark was inspired at an 1889 cakewalk performance done by white men in blackface imitating a southern cook.[11] This drag spectacle was a means by which the white public could satisfy its postslavery desire to prolong the subjugation of Blacks while tantalizing itself with explorations into blackness. Ironically (or perhaps more appropriately, "intentionally"), the reinvented image of Aunt Jemima functions as a similar kind of cultural signifier as the vaudeville performance that inspired the trademark; it recalls and valorizes an oppressive past but in this case using a veneer of culinary respect for black women, while the cakewalk displays a mordant, unabashed mockery of them. The current Aunt Jemima image, which was revamped in the early 1990s to display a less plump and more sophisticated looking woman, does not erase the negative stereotyping that the trademark implies.[12] It simply masks an old sign of hegemonic oppression as a palliative to a new generation of black women.

The Aunt Jemima trademark and its history suggest that black women are haunted from one century into another by an unrelenting racism. They have responded by reinventing themselves from one generation to the next. At times they emerge with straightened hair, bleached skin, and in Western dress, in imitation of their white sisters and in the interests of their safety and security in a racist society. However, their efforts result in them being tyrannized by a physicality that they feel compelled to modify with bleaching creams, frequent salon visits and unrealistic body-image goals.

At other times, in the bleak recognition that their blackness is perceptible whatever disguise they may choose to wear, black women have embraced and flaunted their race, afros and dashikis in tow. These combative efforts are yet another basis for marginalization, demonstrating the insidious nature of hegemonic cultural oppression that in this case isolates acts of black cultural repossession and marks them as signs of the inevitability of racial difference and even as justification for continued racial discrimination.

One such example is the popular "ghetto fabulous" dress culture, which features ornate accessories; erotic, colorful clothing; and elaborate hair fashion. Very different from contemporary Western dress, ghetto fabulous *haute couture* immediately evokes blackness with no apologetic restraint. However, in both black and white communities it has concomitantly become the embodiment of tastelessness, evidence of a disregard for cultural assimilation and the status quo. Undoubtedly those who participate in this fashion trend run the risk of subjecting themselves to the same prejudices as people who have distinctly Afrocentric names and who are routinely rejected as job applicants based solely on the race their name evokes.[13] The resistance to ghetto fabulous dress is in fact less about its perceived tastelessness than about its inherent threat to destabilize racial boundaries.

This kind of cultural censorship was in place a century ago in the British colonies of the Caribbean. In E. A. Hastings' travel narrative *A Glimpse of the Tropics*, published in Britain in 1900, he describes his visit to the town of Mandeville in Jamaica and his encounter with black, Jamaican women dressed for church on Sunday morning.[14] Interestingly, his account from over one hundred years ago parallels today's resistance to ghetto-fabulousness:

> Big hulking negresses were attired in gorgeous silks and satins, and truly wonderful hats with broad brims and feathers, and ribbons of the most elaborate and stylish description. The wooly heads under all this fashionable headgear were pathetically ludicrous. Some had contrived, after years of labour, to gather up a little bunch [of hair] at the back, which gave them an honourable position in negro society. (242)

Hastings' indignation at this superimposing of white dress codes and hair fashion on black bodies and his perception of this act of racial cross-dressing as "ludicrous" reveals his recognition as well as his fear that racial boundaries are unstable. As a deterrence to racial cross-dressing as well as any other attempts to obscure racial boundaries, he links the women's image to Jamaican identity and criticizes their "improper" behavior as representative of every Jamaican of African descent: "We came to the conclusion that Sunday was not the day to see the Jamaica negro in his most pleasing aspect, although the scene was a most comical one" (242). Clearly the "pleasing aspect" of fashion performance that Hastings wishes to view is one that would maintain the illusion of strict racial borders and not betray the constructed nature of whiteness. The comedic value of the scene derives from, in Hastings' view, its unlikeliness; but for us, one hundred years later, there is further comedy in the knowledge that black fashion models are now common fare in the beauty arena.

Fashion has always been instrumental in defining class and concomitantly racial boundaries, and the cumbersome nature of European women's fashion, particularly in the 1800s and 1900s, made it impossible for black and working class white women to engage in economically viable activities while dressed in the latest fashion.[15] Financial constraints were the most apparent barrier, but the clothing's design was yet another restraining factor. Some 1800s dress fashions restrained arm movement and consisted of several layers of clothing that often swept the ground, making it impossible to undertake any but the most limited physical movement.[16]

Black women's historical lack of access to fashion trends, along with perpetuated myths of defeminized black womanhood, contributed to the metaphorical masculinization of black women. Because of the pervasiveness of the Mammy image or myths of a domineering black matriarchy, black femininity has been effaced, consciously and unconsciously, in the interest of white patriarchal control.[17] This process of defeminization has its roots in slavery and provided a "moral" rationale for those engaged in the dehumanization of black women in its myriad forms. Hilary Beckles explains this defeminization within a Caribbean context:

> The black woman was ideologically constructed as essentially "non-feminine" in so far as primacy was placed upon her alleged muscular capabilities,

> physical strength, aggressive carriage, and sturdiness. Pro-slavery writers presented her as devoid of the feminine tenderness and graciousness in which the white woman was tightly wrapped. (Beckles 10)

It is their "feminine tenderness" that black women seek to emphasize with ghetto fabulous fashion in an effort to reconfigure notions of black womanhood.

Ghetto-fabulousness can be read as an effort to inscribe femininity on the black female body. On one level, it seeks to reverse that racist leaching of femininity by overcompensating with exaggerated fashion signifiers. The highly erotic clothing and the expansive portions of the body that this clothing reveals might be seen as an attempt to rebut the suggestion that black womanhood is not feminine. Exposing the black female body assures the presence of physiological femaleness. Furthermore, ghetto fabulous hair fashion subverts hegemonic delineations of femininity by modifying typically white hairstyles, like upswept buns, and by superimposing extensive and elaborate alterations that are meant to suggest an excess of the femininity those styles represent.

This is perhaps the reason why ghetto-fabulousness is predominantly a working-class engagement since the poorest black women in North America experience racism at its most caustic: as both gendered and severe economic oppression. These women's lack of access to education and wealth, the transformative sites from which black women may reduce the effects of racism, increases the extent of their displacement beyond Euro-feminine boundaries. Simultaneously, these women in the lowest socioeconomic brackets experience a greater need to supplement feminine signifiers to compensate for being so displaced from Euro-feminine cultural norms.

However, while ghetto-fabulousness may be empowering to the participants in this fashion trend, it is suspect as an effective compensatory mechanism, not only because of the extensive efforts required to create this look, but because of the subconscious psychosocial motivation it represents, namely an attempt to resituate the black female body within a Euro-feminine realm. Of course, this relocation can never be successfully accomplished because inherent in the desire to resituate black women's bodies is a recognition and ultimately an acceptance of a Eurocentric standard of beauty.

The insidious aspects of comparison at play in this desire to recover the black body must have been significantly affected by the nature of the earliest interaction between black and white women in the West, and the physical locale that best represents that interaction is the plantation great house. It is in this domestic space that black and white women initially had extensive contact with each other in the colonized world, and it is also in this space that they have had to define conflicting yet dependent female identities for themselves. The opposing identity choices black and white women were asked to make were twofold: first they had to understand themselves in Manichean terms as the complete embodiment of virtue and delicacy or as completely unable to achieve either one of those characteristics. Then they had to close this identity gap and share in the consciousness of their joint marginalization in a patriarchal society. Recognizing the potential volatility in black and white female relationships created by this ideological positioning, Minrose C. Gwin ponders the resultant effect: "Placed as they were in an opposing but a similarly dehumanizing mythology, how did the stereotypical sexual roles and obverse images assigned them by white males affect their relationship with one another?" (40). The question is how has black, female identity, especially within a U.S.A. context, been impacted given this history of opposing assumptions regarding womanhood?

Several scholars advocate theories anchored in the conceptualization of difference as the basis for identity formation. Rosalyn Diprose explores gendered physiological difference and recognizes the necessity for female bodies as a defining mirror of contrast in the evolution of a male-centered cultural identity:

> The reproduction of a male ethos as the norm still depends on the exclusion of others. One doesn't have to go far for examples of how female modes of embodiment still cannot easily participate in the body politic without disruption. Pregnant bodies, menstrual bodies, and menopausal bodies have yet to find a comfortable public place. (63)[18]

I would add to Diprose's list of potentially disruptive bodies, fat female bodies, which resist both maleness and assumptions of physiological female normality.

Another theory suggests that differences in socioeconomic positioning are sometimes conveniently explained by conflating constructions of race, gender, and behavioral deviance, and translating these categories into biological differentiations from white male bodies, which are seen as the normative body.[19] All behavioral deviances, and of course the assumption of behavioral deviance that attends constructions of race and gender, are assumed to have a physiological root. Robyn Wiegman expands upon this theory, suggesting that "[M]odernity inaugurates a language concerning difference that increasingly specifies the body as the locus of subjective and social discipline" (48). She refers to white masculinity as "the universal condition of political entitlement" and suggests that the black (or nonwhite) body "anchors the differential meaning of whiteness by lodging it . . . in the epistemology of black skin" (49).

Both Diprose and Wiegman recognize the pivotal function of physiology in the cultural assessment of individuals and in self-perception, and if we are to accept their thesis that difference plays a constitutive role in the formation of identity, femaleness defining maleness, blackness defining whiteness, then my concern is with the ways in which the fat black female body operates in the arena of identity formation. Performing triple duty as an inverse signifier, the fat black woman's body is triply removed from the West's conceptualization of normalcy and situated beyond the outskirts of normative boundaries, which makes its incorporation into the body politic an impossible undertaking. But while the fat, black woman's subject position may be the farthest removed from the white male power center, she also provides an ideal location from which to observe both the machinations of the dominant patriarchy and the convoluted movements of those non-white or non-male bodies engaged in trying to draw nearer to that powerful center.

The fat black woman's body also helps to recreate a parallel beauty arena on the other side of the looking glass. This alternate arena is exclusively populated by black women marginalized by Western beauty standards, and the fat black woman's body assists in the process of defining subcategories of beauty among black women who are excluded from the standards of beauty ascribed for their white counterparts. In these circumstances the fat black woman's body functions as an *evocation* of blackness in a realm where all the bodies are black and there is insufficient racial contrast to provide definition. She denotes a concentrated state of "otherness" relative to hegemonic standards. Thanks to the large black woman, other women of her race can assume the posture of their white counterparts by recognizing themselves to varying degrees as being physiologically what the fat black woman is not.

Although within our current constructions of race there are in fact light-skinned black people whose complexion would appear to provide this contrast, the "appearance" of whiteness does not have the same value as "authentic" whiteness, and once individuals self-perceive themselves as black, their sense of placement in the beauty hierarchy is unquestionably affected. What the fat black woman does is to provide an extreme racial contrast that is situated beyond physiological race in a racial ethos. This contrast is especially useful for darker complexioned women who have no comparable source of racialized physical contrast in the development of their self-identity.

Wiegman suggests that textuality is a redemptive arena where non-white bodies may engage in acts of reclamation, display their acculturation to Western norms and dispel myths of differentiation (63). Fatness and blackness among female characters impact literary rites of repossession, and fat black female bodies function as redefined epicenters of power in the redemptive process and these women's flesh, created through words, becomes the textuality that redefines marginalized people and their sense of powerlessness and resignation (and arguably provides the means for their release from these circumstances).

Alice Randall's controversial novel *The Wind Done Gone* parodies Margaret Mitchell's *Gone With The Wind* (1936) and reconfigures the relationships among the characters to reflect the intricate racial and gender cross-currents of the Civil War era. Mammy is no longer her traditionally asexual self, but actively engaged in a long-term relationship with Planter. Planter owns Cotton Farm, which is the estate where Mammy lives with him, his family and his other slaves. The narrative consists of diary entries written by Cynara, Mammy and Planter's mulatto child. Cynara feels an enormous sense of resentment towards Mammy, whose affections have been disproportionately bestowed upon her charge and Cynara's half-sister, Other, the child of Planter and his wife Lady. And although Cynara is the novel's main character, Mammy is the central identity anchor for all the women in her immediate surroundings at the plantation great house.

As this chapter previously suggested, the black Mammy figure appropriates white women's behavior through its function as an inverse speculum. Mammy quite accurately propagates this blueprint in her relationship to Lady and functions as both a living embodiment of the displacement, or perhaps rather misplacement, blackness represents while constantly supplying Lady with an opposing mile-marker of behavioral territory that she must not occupy. One arena in which the disparity between these two women's roles is starkly presented by Randall is that of sexuality.

Lady's first intimate encounter on her honeymoon night is entirely engineered by Mammy with the assistance of Planter's valet, Garlic. In preparation for the consummation of the marriage, Mammy clandestinely drugs Lady to make her sleep, and when Planter comes to his new wife's bed, Mammy is also there and essentially presents Lady's limp body to Planter, saying, "Do yah bidness and git out" (61). After Planter is done with Lady, Mammy bathes Lady and changes the sheets, leaving her oblivious to any evidence of her first sexual encounter, and Lady assumes that her subsequent pregnancy is an "immaculate conception" (61). The unlikelihood of this incident mocks the Western presumption of sexual modesty and the unrealistic perception of perpetual chastity among white women by subverting these presumptions of feminized white asexuality that contrast with the aura of promiscuity that has come to define black female sexuality. This black promiscuity is the next stereotype that the novel caricatures since immediately following Lady's non-sexual/sexual encounter, Mammy goes to Planter's room, where she "gave him what he wanted in his bed. She gave it so good, he never complained" (61).

Mammy's actions underscore her ability to covertly influence Lady's behavior. She surreptitiously directs Lady's romantic choices and all but provides her with written instructions indicating whom she should marry. As Lady's slave she recognizes the potential for abuse and the curtailment of what freedom she has if she ends up on the wrong plantation. So along with Garlic, who is similarly concerned about his future, Mammy orchestrates Lady's marriage to Planter because of the beneficial absence of any immediate family members and the isolated placement of his plantation. Garlic explains: "If Lady married a man on a lonely place, a man with no people, Pallas [Mammy] could run the place and she'd be free, free as she was going to be" (60). And so while Lady, who is only fifteen at the time, is distraught over the death of a previous love, Mammy engages in a reverse psychological maneuver by introducing opposing but by no means mutually exclusive choices to Lady—joining a convent or marrying Planter—and succeeds in getting her way (61).

Blackness is further situated as a defining entity of whiteness on an economic plane with the symbolic installment of both Mammy and Garlic as the de facto mistress and master of Cotton Farm. Years after Cynara returns to the plantation at the time of Mammy's death, Garlic explains the origins of Cotton Farm and how he poisoned his old master and fixed a card game so that Planter could win him and enough money to purchase property (64). Garlic's role in the acquisition of the estate subverts myths of superior white entrepreneurial skills, competency, and hard work as the source of white economic prowess and relocates the source of that wealth as the black labor that created it.

Mammy's body also operates as the embodiment of otherness and one element of her alterity is situated in her appearance in contrast to Lady's. Mammy is fat and described as being "big as an elephant with tiny dark round eyes" (6). And her strength, encrypted in the elephantine portrayal of her appearance, is reinforced by added descriptions of her hands as having "strong-as-branches fingers" (6). In comparison, Lady is described by Cynara in opposing terms as being delicate and pale: "Lady's tidy, tiny, sweet-smelling self, her slight but supple arms, the white, heaven-pillow bosom that lay corseted beneath Lady's modest gowns, brought sweat to my brow" (102). Mammy's breasts are large, symbolizing the multiple ways in which she had to give of herself, maternally to her daughter, Cynara, and her charge, Other, and sexually to Planter. In a diary entry, Cynara's description of how Other interacts with Mammy indicates how Mammy's breasts and her fat function metaphorically as a source of emotional nurture: "Other rested her head on Mammy's brown pillow breasts, snuggled in beneath a blanket of fat brown arm, breathed in the prayer of Mammy's breath and out the god of her presence" (7).

Quite appropriately it is in this arena of maternal symbolism that we are able to observe the complexities of plantation identity politics unfold as Mammy becomes the mother figure with whom Other strongly identifies while Cynara and Lady form a bond, joined together on the periphery of the great house. Through separate incidents involving the two mother-daughter pairs living in the plantation house we can observe the complexities of race and gender constructions. In both incidents the maternal breast and its accessibility and desirability reconfigure the mother-daughter pairings across racial boundaries. The result is racially inconsistent mother-daughter couplings that quite appropriately represent the psychic mother-daughter configurations at play if we construe the mother as a defining gauge of identity.

In the first incident Other, who is about three years old, walks past Lady and Cynara, who is also about the same age, to insist upon access to Mammy's breast:

> Other reached into the top of Mammy's dress and pulled out my mother's breast. "I want some titty-tip," She said, and I ached in some place I didn't know I had, where my heart should have been but wasn't . . . I flushed in a rage of possession as those little white hands drew the nipple toward the little pink mouth, then clasped on. (13)

From their early childhood an ongoing competition develops between Cynara and Other, ostensibly for the privilege of Mammy's affection but in fact for a validation of each girl's identity and cultural value. While Other has the benefit of Mammy's presence as a demarcation of black versus white womanhood, Cynara must struggle to understand what she means to both Mammy and Planter. Eventually Planter sells her to alleviate Other's discomfort over the sexual competition Cynara presents.

In response to this betrayal, Cynara engages in a lifelong love affair with Other's husband, trying to undo her experience of maternal marginalization and paternal dispossession. When Cynara is sent from Cotton Farm to be sold, she is given an accompanying letter written by her father. The letter is directed to one of Planter's acquaintances explaining the circumstances surrounding Cynara's sale and requesting that the acquaintance refrain from abusing her too severely. In later years when Cynara is able to read and she comprehends the content of the letter, she writes: "Twice I've been kilt by a man. Once was when I read Planter's words on paper" (37). Cynara's confounded status as a mulatto suggests a pastiche quality to the novel as a replay of the tragic mulatto plot; however, Mammy's centrality as a producer of white identity, as well as Cynara's complex relationship with Lady, gives this story an unusual twist.

Mammy economizes on the dispensation of her affections, favoring the more lucrative object for her warmth—Other—whose race and class privileges will help in the continued accommodation of Mammy's surreptitious control of the plantation. In one entry Cynara writes: "By the time we were born, choosing between Other and me was like choosing between paper dolls, and Other had the prettier clothes" (54). As a result, Cynara experiences tremendous resentment and jealousy because she is displaced from her role as daughter and further displaced from the experience of white, and hence authentic, womanhood because of her race. Ironically Lady also experiences displacement, but it is from her role as mother. The result is that Cynara and Lady create a compensatory pseudo-maternal bond, allowing each to perform in the role she was denied. Cynara explains: "I looked and wanted to suck; Lady looked and wanted to suckle-feed. We were both envious." Later that evening as Lady prepares for her bath she orders Mammy to send Cynara to her with some milk (15). To Cynara's surprise Lady offers to share the glass of sweet milk and then proffers her breast while Cynara helps her to undress:[20]

> Her bared breast was just a little thing with a dented nipple almost as big as the circle it stood in. The circle was that tiny. [Lady asks,] "Are you still hungry?" I nodded again.
>
> She pulled me onto her lap and I suckled at her breast till her warm milk filled me. . . . We had been sharing these little spurred-by-envy suppers all my memory, but each time the milk came and how long it came without running out was a mystery to us both. Later when I slept beside her she said, "You're my little girl, aren't you?" (16)

Even after Mammy's death, when both Cynara and Other are grown women, Cynara struggles to make peace with Mammy and Other's relationship. Cynara writes that after Mammy's funeral service "Other was awarded pride of place at the head of the line of mourners. I was to follow right behind." During this march back to the house Other chastises Cynara for neglecting Mammy. This act reinforces the tyranny of the racist gender constructions Cynara must navigate since the object of Mammy's displaced attention is empowered to critique Cynara's response to the pain that source helped to create. In response to this pain Cynara continues to find refuge in Lady, who has already died; Cynara writes, "I went back in the house, sneaked into Lady's room, crawled into our bed, and cried" (54).

Mammy's size is configured as a cogent symbol of her productive capacity on multiple planes—as a laborer, as clandestine mistress of Cotton Farm, and as an identity anchor. Unlike Lady, whose corset restrains her but leaves her appearing "tidy," the grandness of Mammy's resources work together to enable her position of power (102). As Cynara tries to make peace with Mammy and their dysfunctional mother-daughter relationship, she contemplates her significance relative to Mammy's size, hoping that she is a product of those resources: "I wondered if her love of bigness, the pleasure she took in being immense, had anything to do with a love of carrying me. I hoped that it did" (40). Furthermore Mammy's fat is a shield from the effects of slavery's oppression and the emotional repercussion of Other's eventual withdrawal from Mammy: "Mammy gained fifty pounds one year, forty the next, twenty the year after that, and the slight, barely hundred-pound body in which she had walked into the house and slipped into Planter's bed vanished beneath another hundred pounds of protective flesh" (101).

Cynara does not have this cushion, as her body is small and tidy like Lady's (72). Additionally, her relationship with her lover, R.—Other's husband—prevents her from having this buffer as it would not meet with his approval. On the other hand, Garlic, who recognizes the essential value of aligning with someone as resourceful as Mammy, has an appreciation for her size. Of Garlic, Cynara writes: "he liked his women with great big legs. If I ever started to get big, R. would let me go" (6).

Despite the difference between Garlic's taste in women compared to that of the white hegemony embodied by R., he and Planter comfortably inhabit the same patriarchal territory. Like Planter, Garlic has sex with Mammy, and Garlic even thinks he might be Cynara's father until she is born with unmistakably biracial features (59). Additionally, he is able to surreptitiously beguile Planter into listening to his ideas, symbolically merging their authorial postures and locating both black and white men in the same realm of intention. Garlic explains: "All I could see to lifting me up was pulling real close to a powerful man and teasing him into thinking my thoughts was his own," further suggesting that Garlic and Planter dwell in similar psychic locations (60).

But the most significant indicator that he and Planter occupy parallel hierarchical spaces that subsume Cynara's agency and her opportunity to in some way inherit the patriarchal mantle of power is the gift of Planter's watch to Garlic (50). Interestingly it is not left for him by Planter but handed over by Other, who feels Garlic most deserves this possession of her father's. Other's choice is a potent simulation of how the construction of white womanhood depends upon the perpetuation of sexist gender ideology that secures the white woman's post as the fairer, more restrained and delicate sex. Passing on the heirloom to Cynara would authorize her existence and legitimacy in ways that subvert definitions of white womanhood.

The novel also extends its forays into the arena of identity politics through its allegorical naming conventions. The use of generic terms not usually assigned to specific individuals accomplishes two things: First, it replicates the hegemonic impulse to amalgamate marginalized peoples through stereotypes and through the use of generic names such as "Uncle" and "Mammy." By extending that practice to Whites in the novel, attention is drawn to the indistinct quality each name assumes, thereby blurring the identifying parameters associated with each character. Additionally, Randall creates room for us to imagine that her characters are those from *Gone With The Wind* without having to distinctly state so. This sort of indeterminate subject position she creates provides reinforcement of and draws attention back to the challenges of Cynara's circumstances and the identity limbo in which she has been forced to dwell.

Like Cynara, the novel also endured identity limbo when the publication of *The Wind Done Gone* was delayed because of a lawsuit brought against Randall's publishers by Margaret Mitchell's Trust.[21] Mitchell's estate contended that Randall's novel impinged upon their copyright of *Gone With The Wind*.[22] But on the other hand, because Randall was always troubled by Mitchell's depiction of Blacks in *Gone With The Wind*, she seeks to explore beyond the narrow racial confines of Mitchell's work.[23] Two months into the court battle, the Mitchell Trust agreed to terminate their litigation without relinquishing the assumption that their legal posture was justified, and they required that the novel be subtitled "An Unauthorized Parody."[24] Additionally, the Mitchell Trust retains the right to legally intervene in any further productive attempts such as a television sequel or a motion picture.[25]

The requirement that the novel be labeled "An Unauthorized Parody" is a fitting metaphor for the hegemonic response to any assumptions of independent black identity. Not only is this identity rendered inauthentic but also a comedic mutation of the real thing.[26] Nevertheless, the term "parody" does suggest a covert method of invalidating the original. This literary legal drama demonstrates the consequence of attempts to reclaim or reconfigure black identity.[27]

Tsitsi Dangarembga's *Nervous Conditions* also explores this issue of black identity, and Nyasha, a secondary protagonist in the novel, is destabilized as she tries to navigate between gendered Western constructions of beauty and identity and those of her native African culture. She has been raised in both Britain and Africa, and her bifurcated identity leads to a grave eating disorder and subsequently a bout of mental illness. The novel is a bildungsroman set in Rhodesia (pre-independent Zimbabwe) and narrated by a young female protagonist, Tambudzai. Tambu, as she is called, is smart and academically ambitious, and through a combination of her own efforts as well of the serendipitous death of her older brother she ends up being taken under the wings of an educated uncle, Babamukuru. Tambu's uncle, who attended university in England and is a school principal, takes her to live with him and his family and sponsors the remainder of her secondary education. During the time with her uncle Tambu reestablishes a friendship with her cousin Nyasha (Babamukuru's daughter), and it is via Tambu's observations of her cousin's behavior that Nyasha's dysfunctional relationship with food unfolds. While Nyasha never becomes fat, her fear of physiological fatness as well as the food that might lead to this state offers an alternate route for investigating the role of body size and identity in the Diaspora.[28]

Although *Nervous Conditions* deprives us of the opportunity to share the fat black woman's perspective on her world and to observe her role in identity creation for those around her, we are privy to one character's obsession with the fat black woman. Nyasha is consumed with thoughts of fatness that underlie her recognition of the large black woman's identity as situated beyond the parameters of normalized Western identity. Because Nyasha lacks a stable sense of herself, she fluctuates between assuming an African identity, grounded in her Shona tribal culture, and a Western identity, learned during her stay in Britain. As a result, she obsesses over this figure of the fat black woman that embodies the sense of otherness that is a vital component of her identity crisis. On one hand Nyasha wishes to reject a Eurocentric selfhood that locates her in marginalized identity terrain based on hegemonic constructions of race. On the other hand she is reluctant to embrace African selfhood that marginalizes her because of her gender. Because of this inverse binary, Nyasha ends up overwhelmed by the very image she is rejecting, and although she never puts on weight, she is pertinent to my discussion of the fat black woman's role in the creation of identity. The fat black woman is eventually all that Nyasha thinks about as she slowly starves herself into oblivion—effacing her body in an effort to efface her problematic identity.

Nyasha's eventual breakdown and eating disorder partially result from her resistance to certain behavioral norms of Shona society, a resistance which in some respects was clearly facilitated and encouraged by her parents, who exposed her to European culture and education. Thus, food becomes a dominating symbol in Nyasha's struggle. Although any relationship between eating disorders and colonization seems quite unlikely, comments from the Anorexia Nervosa and Bulimia Association suggests otherwise. They list the fear of falling under someone else's control and apprehensions over one's own lack of domination as some of the several influential components of anorexia.[29]

The destabilization of Nyasha's identity was initiated when her father, Babamukuru, along with his wife and children, went off to England for five years for him to complete his education. Upon returning to Africa, Nyasha's disconnection from Rhodesian culture is immediately apparent to Tambu when Babamukuru, his wife, Maiguru, and their children come to visit Tambu's family: "[Maiguru] did not look as though she had been to England. My cousin Nyasha, pretty bright Nyasha, on the other hand, obviously had. There was no other explanation for the tiny little dress she wore, hardly enough of it to cover her thighs" (37). As the visit progresses, it becomes more apparent that Nyasha and her brother have been displaced from their native culture. This displacement is exemplified when Tambu invites Nyasha to dance only to have Maiguru explain that Nyasha no longer understands their native Shona language since all she has spoken for the last five years is English (42). Furthermore, Maiguru discourages her daughter's involvement in the dance ritual even though the young girl appears interested in participating, and eventually Maiguru declines Tambu's invitation on Nyasha's behalf (42).

After Tambu goes to live with her uncle and his family, she recognizes the extent of this tension between the influences of British versus African culture. On the first evening Tambu dines with Babamukuru and his family, there is an altercation between Nyasha and her father at the dinner table. The row is initiated when Babamukuru realizes that his daughter is reading *Lady Chatterley's Lover*: "Babamukuru was distressed, looking sad, then hurt, then ultimately annoyed. 'Tss!' he shook his head. 'I don't know what's wrong with our daughter. She has no sense of decency, none whatsoever'" (81). During this discussion Nyasha is not at the table as she has gotten up to make some gravy that the housekeeper forgot to prepare. Maiguru, who has already served a plate of food for her husband, unsuccessfully tries to plead on her daughter's behalf, but Babamukuru confiscates the book without Nyasha's knowledge.

By the time that Nyasha returns to the table with the gravy, Maiguru, fearing that Babamukuru's food has gotten cold, decides that she will eat his cold plate of food herself, and she starts to prepare him a fresh plate. Nyasha, tired of waiting for Maiguru to finish, begins to serve her own food before her mother is finished preparing Babamukuru's new plate. When her father questions Nyasha's disruption of the serving ritual by taking her food before he has gotten his, she responds by saying that she does not want her food to get cold.

The culmination of this episode at the dinner table situates food as a currency for power and becomes a poignant signifier as Nyasha becomes aware that she is powerless and that one of the few arenas in which she can assert some control over her actions is with regard to when and how she eats.[30] As dinner progresses and Nyasha realizes that her father has impounded her book, she voices her disagreement, first arguing with Babamukuru then storming away from the table:

> "Now where are you going?" Babamukuru demanded.
> "To my bedroom," replied Nyasha.
> "What did you say?" Cried Babamukuru, his voice crackling in disbelief.

> "Didn't you hear me tell you I don't want to hear you answer back? Didn't you hear me tell you that just now? Now sit down and eat that food. All of it. I want to see you eat all of it."
>
> "I've had enough," explained Nyasha. "Really, I'm full." Her foot began to tap. Instead of sitting down she walked out of the dining-room. (83–84)

By not eating she defeminizes herself, becoming slender and hence less attractive within the context of Shona beauty aesthetics.[31] Additionally, her decline in physical appeal translates into a diminution in her economic value as a marriageable female, who attracts a dowry.[32]

Babamukuru's insistence that Nyasha eat and maintain her gendered value is at odds with his resistance to her earlier efforts to attend to her hunger by promptly feeding herself and privileging her own demands for food. This conflicted patriarchal posture creates diametrically opposing behavioral requirements for Nyasha and sets the stage for her subsequent mental deterioration. Furthermore, the family's European diet symbolizes the conflicting spaces that Nyasha's parents expect her to occupy. They have exposed her to British culture, provided her with a European education, but yet require her to disregard the desires that result from that exposure. Nyasha must digest the food that symbolizes this exposure but remain immune to that food's transformative effects on her system. The contradictory character of these requirements with regard to the symbolic assimilation of food foreshadows Nyasha's impending identity crisis.

Some of the other Shona women have a far less problematic relationship with food. Tambu's Aunt Lucia is a resourceful and sexually independent woman who "had managed somehow to keep herself plump in spite of her tribulations" (127). Lucia, who sleeps with whomever she wants and is impervious to gossip about her sexuality, eventually enrolls herself in an adult education program and is thoroughly pleased with her new potential for progress (127, 186). Another of Tambu's aunts is Tete Gladys, a particularly large woman whose size is emblematic of her status in the family:

> The cars rolled to a stop beneath the mango trees. Tete Gladys disembarked with difficulty, with false starts and strenuous breathing because she was so large . . . her mass was not frivolous. It had a ponderous presence which rendered any situation, even her attempts to remove herself from her car, weighty and serious. We did not giggle, did not think of it. (36)

Although Tete Gladys is much more respected among the family than Lucia, like Lucia she is also secure in her identity, chiding Maiguru when she discourages her children from dancing, and participating in family discussions as much as her brothers (43–47). Her comfort with her body and herself is further obvious as she dances at Babamukuru's welcome gathering: "Tete Gladys, arms swinging, dress swishing was on her feet, swirling dizzily left and right to the tempo of 'Amazing Grace,' executing an exuberant bow at the end of each bar" (42). Furthermore, because Tete Gladys has been given "patriarchal status," she is exempt from some of the usual women's work when the family gathers for holidays (133).

On the other hand the novel constructs the slender bodies of Maiguru (Tambu's aunt) and Mainini (Tambu's mother) as metonyms for oppression under the tyranny of Eurocentric idealism. Maiguru is dominated by her husband and her speech reflects an almost childlike posture when she refers to Babamukuru as her "Daddy-dear" and "Daddy-pie" (80). Maiguru's subservience as well as Dangarembga's clever narrative construction leaves the reader assuming that Maiguru could not possibly have the same educational status as Babamukuru; however, in a conversation with Tambu, Maiguru reveals that like her husband she also has a Master's degree and earns an income that helps support the family: "When I was in England," Maiguru wistfully explains, "I glimpsed for a little while the things I could have been, the things I could have done if—if—if things were different" (101). In many ways Maiguru is subject to the same tyrannies as her daughter, but she chooses to ignore potentially complicating desires. She does this to safeguard her husband's identity, rooted in his dominance, and to situate herself in the comfortable and familiar role of devoted wife. Tambu supports her aunt's resolve: "if it was necessary to efface yourself in order to preserve his sense of identity and value, then, I was sure, Maiguru had taken the correct decisions" (102).[33]

Unlike her mother, Tambu eats well and even gains weight while living in her uncle's household. Once Tambu settles into her new life in her uncle's home and has access to the education she has always craved, embodied by the extensive availability of food in her uncle's household, Tambu not only gains weight but begins to menstruate. This onset of her menses suggests that her fat is not only the physiological trigger for her period to begin, but a symbol of her personal fulfillment, and this is what transports her into womanhood (95).

Nyasha's menstrual cycle and her appetite are also linked to the integrity of her self-perception. In the days that follow a tumultuous fight between Nyasha and her father over her appropriate conduct as a girl, Nyasha stops eating and begins to grow ill (118). Days later Nyasha confides in Tambu about the emotional turbulence she is experiencing in the wake of the fight and allows herself to grieve over the event. The following day when she wakes up, she feels much better, and although it is nine days early, her period begins, signaling the metaphoric presence of fat—her recovering sense of self—as a facilitator of growth (119). The waning of Nyasha's appetite is also linked to her loss of identity and control over her life as well as the experience of neocolonialism.

One day when Babamukuru commands Nyasha to finish eating, naming himself as the source of her sustenance, Nyasha's eating disorder rapidly spirals downward, nearing its nadir (189). Babamukuru is the embodiment of Eurocentrism by virtue of both his religious affiliation with the missionaries and his British education. This association between Babamukuru and Western consciousness highlights Nyasha's own hybrid identity dilemma, and the concluding bulimic episode when she makes herself vomit is a cogent symbolic rejection of both patriarchy and Eurocentrism. Eventually Nyasha becomes even more emaciated as she prepares for her O levels and studies up to fourteen hours per day while the family is on vacation. Then early one morning in an incoherent outburst she begins mincing her history books between her teeth, literally conflating both food and knowledge as she had metaphorically done all along[34]: "'Their history. Fucking liars. Their bloody lies. . . . They've trapped us. They've trapped us. But I won't be trapped. I'm not a good girl. I won't be trapped" (201). Additionally, she claws at her own body with fragments of a clay pot she has destroyed, her efforts meant to disembody herself and hence obliterate her identity, the source of her torment. In her final words before she passes out after her outburst, she explains to her mother, "Look what they've done to us. . . . I'm not one of them but I'm not one of you" (201).

Unlike Nyasha, who eats too little, one of the main characters in Joan Riley's novel *Romance*, overindulges in food, literally binging her way through most of the novel. Set in London, *Romance*, like *Nervous Conditions,* features two closely bonded women as dual protagonists, each one's body reflecting a different relationship with food. The women are sisters of Caribbean descent—Verona is robust and single and lives with her older sister Desiree, who is slender, sickly, and married with two children. The household, already destabilized by Desiree's illness and her husband John's chauvinistic demands, is further unbalanced when Verona loses her job. Tricked into confessing to theft at her workplace when she did not in fact commit the crime, Verona is ashamed to reveal her job loss to her sister and pretends that all is well and she is still employed. However, as the novel progresses we learn that there is yet another traumatic event affecting Verona: at fourteen she was raped by one of Desiree's boyfriends, but she never told anyone about this incident, and although she is now twenty-seven, Verona has not recovered from this assault which is at the root of her overeating (19).

Throughout *Romance* Verona tries to escape from her identity as a fat black woman by immersing herself in the fictitious world of skinny, white heroines found in the romance novels she feverishly reads. One problematic element of the identity from which Verona tries to escape is her vulnerability, most evident to her through her rape. Another is the fragile social space she occupies based on her ethnic identity, and this space becomes particularly apparent through the racial underpinnings of the conspiracy among her white superiors that eventually leads to her losing her job. Uncomfortable with the constraints of the racial and gendered space her large black female body forces her to occupy, Verona uses her romance novel fantasies to transport her from those realities dictated by her physiology. For example, on the evening after two company officials visit Verona's home to confront her about the fabricated robbery at her workplace, she buries herself in the anguish of her novel's characters instead of confronting her own pain. Verona reads to herself from one of her novels:

> She stared helplessly into the compelling depths of the strange grey eyes, feeling little quivers of nerves in the pit of her stomach as he moved forward with grim determination. "How can I let you go, chérie?" . . .
>
> Verona shifted to a more comfortable position on the sagging mattress as she came to the end of the page and turned the leaf slowly. . . . The earlier trauma of the day temporarily forgotten, Verona was totally immersed in the role of the beautiful blonde heroine, her whole being transported to the French countryside and the tall, dark, handsome count. (17)

Verona's life seems far removed from those of her romance novel characters; however, she is unaware that her identity is an integral component of those fictitious white identities that she craves.

In *Romance,* whiteness becomes a defining index for Verona's identity since it is situated as the ideal and the opposite of Verona's life. In the world of romance novels, those slender, white female bodies are associated with effortless wealth, unparalleled beauty and infinite romance while Verona perceives her physical identity to be defined by her life's attendant trauma. Her large black body is located in a space overwhelmed by racism, sexism, and poverty and is such a remarkable evocation of otherness that Verona continuously attempts to relocate into otherwise defined spaces to alleviate her distress. Both her romance novels and her practice of exclusively dating white men achieve this temporary reprieve for her.

Verona has made this choice because she associates black masculinity with Desiree's boyfriend who raped her. Additionally, her boyfriends are generally older married men like Guy, the man she is dating at the opening of the novel, since the emotional distance created by the difference in age along with these men's unavailability make the relationship more tolerable for Verona:

> As far as Des knew, Verona's interest in things sexual was limited to the romances she read so avidly. But how could Des understand the nightmares that still haunted her, or that out-of-control feeling that younger or more aggressive men—black men—gave her?

> She realized that men like Guy were fascinated by her skin, finding the colour and texture alien and exotic. They were flattered by her attention. With them she was in control and could indulge her fantasy. (18–19)

However, Verona fails in her tentative efforts to inscribe an escape identity through an association with white male bodies. For example, she is ashamed of the men she dates, forbidding them to visit her at home out of fear of what Desiree may think, and when Guy telephones her one evening because of a sudden change of plans, she bursts into an outraged fit telling him never to call her there again (19). This inability to comfortably connect with her white boyfriends betrays Verona's subconscious awareness that the motivation for her relationships is misguided and grounded in unsettling presumptions about herself—specifically her race and gender.

Furthermore, Verona's relationships result in a constant replay of the rape because she does not sincerely find these older men to be desirable. Upon seeing Guy on one occasion when they meet for a date, Verona is immediately affected by his appearance: "Guy was waiting for her outside the usual pub, waving madly as the bus sped past to the stop a few yards on. . . . She felt depressed as she noticed his sagging trousers and overflowing stomach" (73). Additionally, their intimacy is hindered by her revulsion towards him: "She leaned closer to him, avoiding the wispy grey hairs that made no attempt to cover his scalp, and steeling herself for the slightly unwashed smell that always clung to him" (74). Guy's gray hair and unpleasant body odor both impede Verona's efforts at physical contact and are emblematic of the emotional barriers prohibiting intimacy in the relationship and defeating her efforts to escape from herself.

Overeating, for Verona, is another form of diversion from the realities of her existence, and she especially enjoys binging on candy. Her penchant suggests the desire to revisit her childhood, the time in her life when she was violated, perhaps in an effort to recapture an age of innocence before the rape. Verona is particularly drawn to candy during those times when the painful reality of her identity besieges her. For example, one morning as Verona prepares for work, her young niece, who is being scolded for not eating her breakfast, explains that she does not want to become fat like Verona: "Some of the girls at school say you look like the Michelin man, Auntie V," the child tells her aunt (33).

Shortly after this incident as Verona walks to work, she daydreams that she is in the scene of one of her romance novels, playing the role of leading lady and walking down a lane in the Spanish countryside, enveloped by the warm sun (34). However, in actuality Verona is in London in the middle of winter walking across a frozen landscape (34). As a result of her reverie she almost steps into dog poop, and she walks in front of a moving vehicle. She eventually composes herself and continues her journey to work; however, when she reaches the shop where she usually purchases her stash of candy for the day, she orders even more boxes than usual as well as a bottle of soda (36). Symbolically she packs her candy in the same bag that stores her books, marking these two sets of items as sharing the same function of facilitating a getaway from herself (36). This series of events reinforces the disparity between Verona's lived and imagined identities and assists in displacing her from the subject position she craves since she chooses to assuage her discomfort with food. Verona's large body is the result of eating binges meant to assuage her pain but that further remove her from the idyllic world of the svelte leading ladies in her books.[35]

Eventually Verona becomes acquainted with a young white man, and their relationship holds the promise of finally providing Verona with her personal storybook romance. She meets Steve at the benefits office, and she is awestruck by his "unruly blond hair," "his honey-gold moustache," and his "boyish grin" (170). As a matter of fact, Verona is so excited about what she perceives as her real life entrance into the fictitious world of romance that her relationship with Steve displaces the novels she constantly reads as well as her binging sprees:

> She was walking on air. . . .What did it matter that she had to cancel her romance subscription from lack of money, or that the books in the library were ones she had already read? Even the fact that she had lost five whole pounds in weight seemed small potatoes now.
>
> She had met *him*. (170)

The books and the candy are no longer necessary since Steve takes their place as a potent means of conveyance into a matrix of romantic myth, and Verona's enthusiasm over her new relationship is accounted for by Steve's efficient ability to assist her in creating an illusory identity. Steve has more of the physiological qualities that liken him to the leading men in Verona's novels: his rugged handsomeness and youth as well as his status as a bachelor suggest greater marketability than men like Guy whose desperation may make them less discriminating in their relationships. Consequently, Verona's choice to date Steve better resembles the relationships of her romance novel heroines.

Moreover, Steve is a writer and his status as the creator of those fictitious worlds that Verona inhabits further excites her while imbuing him with a measure of divinity (171). The trope of the romantic novel is employed in the narrative structure of *Romance*, and the language Riley uses to describe Verona and Steve's first sexual encounter mimics the narrative style of formulaic romance stories. "Steve started to touch her, clumsily exploring her loose bulk under the pink cotton sundress . . ." and other lines such as "She ran her fingers through his untidy blond hair, along his narrow back and flat bottom . . ." are mirrored reflections emanating from the same fictitious world that helps Verona to navigate her environment with regard to identity (173, 174). However, Verona's euphoria over her relationship with Steve is evanescent, and like all of her other escape ventures, the union fails to fulfill her ultimate desire of re-designating her identity.

To begin with, Steve is not as charming as Verona initially believes him to be, and interspersed in his ostensibly innocuous introduction of himself to Verona on the first day they meet is the wry suggestion that their intellectual capacities are unevenly matched:

> "I'm an accounts clerk," she said warily, adding shyly: "What about you?"
> He grinned. "I'm a writer. Technically I ain't really unemployed, but I need some bread while I work on my book."
> . . . "I bet your book's gonna be great. I'm going to buy it as soon as it get finish."
> "You couldn't read stuff like mine," his voice had a faint edge of contempt; but he was smiling, and somehow nothing else mattered. (171)

Aside from denigrating Verona's mental capacity, Steve's comment foreshadows the painful turn their relationship eventually takes by suggesting that he will not participate in her illusory fairytale enactments. His comment that Verona is unable to "read stuff like [his]" implies a communication rift symbolized by the language incompatibility between them, and since Verona's identity is precariously balanced on the back of words, this rift does not bode well for her.

Their first sexual encounter also indicates an undercurrent of imbalance. It takes place during Verona's initial visit to Steve's messy apartment and is preceded by her extensively cleaning his flat while he sits around, supposedly for the purpose of keeping out of her way (172). To help make the experience more palatable, Verona superimposes one of her romance novels on her situation: "It was just like in *Concertina Love,* she recalled, where Alain went into decline and April found him in squalor when his mother urged her to visit him. Verona felt happier thinking of it in that context" (172). Although this application of a romantic veneer reduces Verona's discomfort over tidying Steve's apartment, her domestic labor and sexuality remain awkwardly intertwined, and Steve's sexual acknowledgment of Verona is dependent on her domestic capability, since it is when she finishes cleaning that he praises her for the fine job she has done and then proceeds to seduce her (173).

She is excited about this encounter and surrenders quite willingly, but when it is all over, her dissatisfaction and uneasiness are apparent: "Afterwards, she felt aching and unfulfilled, thinking longingly of the bath she had scrubbed back to whiteness" (174). Verona's memory of Steve's grimy bath that her efforts have made pristine alludes to her own sense of being sexually besmirched, initially by the rape, and time and time again by the men with whom she sleeps, and although her enthusiasm over Steve is unique among her relationships, it still evokes the specter of her childhood assault. She eventually asks Steve if she can take a bath, solidifying her sense of being dirty and her desire to symbolically share in the same rites of renewal and reappropriation as the dirty tub she just cleaned.

Verona employs various romantic myths to camouflage her blemished identity, but all are eventually disrupted by some material encounter with herself that unmistakably resituates her as a fat black woman, and the most disruptive of such engagements takes place when she discovers she is pregnant.[36] Ashamed to stay with her sister, Verona arrives on Steve's doorsteps, suitcases in hand, only to find that he is not at all welcoming towards her (213). Circumstances deteriorate even further when she tells him that she is pregnant and he assaults her, kicking her in the stomach and saying, "I don't want no black bastard calling me Dad" (214). Steve's scathing comment and his symbolically abortive action emphasize that because of her blackness Verona is beyond the realm of white male protection offered to her romance heroines. This event forcefully resituates Verona's sense of herself in the racialized and gendered world in which she lives.

It is Verona's condition of pregnancy that finally completes this process of disengagement from the make-believe world of romance. All the physiological forms of otherness that already attend Verona are further underscored by her pregnancy.[37] And it is during the course of her pregnancy, as her body becomes further marginalized, that Verona finally starts to come to terms with her true self. Steve's assault painfully reiterates the absence of romance in her life and after that abusive episode she vows to refrain from any more relationships with white men (214). This decision implies that Verona can now perceive the superficiality of the veneer of comfort provided by these relationships and that she is ready to work through her anger and resentment associated with black men. Additionally, she is finally able to tell Desiree about the rape, letting go of the shame associated with the event, a shame that she felt forced to keep as a secret all these years (224).

Romance, like *Nervous Conditions* and *The Wind Done Gone*, explores the creation of identity among black women and suggests that constructions of whiteness and blackness exist in tension with each other—each the speculum necessary to reflect meaning to the other. Both *Romance* and *Nervous Conditions* offer relatively disempowered responses to the historical Mammy image compared to Randall's more defiant response in *The Wind Done Gone*. The insulated nature of the plantation in Randall's work as well as the limited opportunities for media influence during that chronological period are significant contributors to Mammy's fearless governance of herself and the plantation. *Romance* and *Nervous Conditions* speak to the ways in which technology has intervened in the creation of culture and identity. Through both travel and the exposure to writing crafted with Western paradigms, both Verona and Nyasha become incredibly disenchanted with their bodies because their cultural encounters with the West (in this case Europe) have invalidated their bodies in some way. As a result Nyasha and Verona are embroiled in a struggle to comfortably position themselves within a Eurocentric beauty arena, and they both resist the sociopolitical consequences of occupying their racialized and gendered bodies.

Despite the diverse emotional territory these characters occupy, they all proffer some degree of textual redemption for bodies such as theirs, bodies marginalized by race, gender and Western beauty standards. The texts discussed in this chapter imply that fatness and blackness are characteristics that strategically situate women in positions that facilitate the reconsideration of a Eurocentric beauty aesthetic in a plural society and encourage a reconceptualization of how we construct race and gender. Nyasha and Verona, who seek to escape from their identities (real or imagined) as fat black women, both suffer emotional trauma as a result of their efforts. Their distress suggests that the identities which they wish to escape are meaningful since any attempt to displace these identities creates imbalance. On the other hand, Mammy, who comfortably occupies her large body, is an icon of cunning and ingeniousness, implying that her surreptitious dominance over the plantation is associated with her "love of bigness" (Randall 40).

NOTES

1. See my initial use of this term in the introduction.
2. Patricia Hill Collins, *Black Feminist Thought: Knowledge, Consciousness and the Politics of Empowerment* (New York: Routledge, Chapman and Hall, Inc., 1991), 71.
3. Although the Mammy figure emerged within the context of the United States (see Collins, *Black Feminist Thought*, 71), I find this icon paradigmatic for the African Diaspora because of the similar Western aesthetic values held by the European colonizing forces responsible for the post-Colombian expansion of black slavery.
4. Collins, *Black Feminist Thought*, 78.
5. Collins, *Black Feminist Thought*, 67.
6. Patricia Morton, *Disfigured Images: The Historical Assault on Afro-American Women* (New York: Greenwood Press, 1991), 9.

7. Morton, *Disfigured Images*, 6–7. See Morton for a detailed discussion of Mammy's role in creating gendered, intraracial rivalry.

8. Collins, *Black Feminist Thought*, 72.

9. I use "postcolonial" to refer to various regions that were at one point occupied during the numerous colonizing ventures that sprang from Christopher Columbus's voyages and subsequent "discoveries." These regions include the Caribbean and Africa; however, I also conceive of the United States as a postcolonial site—not in the context of white immigrants and their British colonial overseers but in terms of African Americans and these various groups of white immigrants, who eventually became colonial overseers themselves. I envision the Unites States as a country in which the colonized were subjugated on the same geographic territory their colonizers called home instead of in the homeland of those being exploited as was the case in Africa, or in a third party location as was the case in the Caribbean. I certainly acknowledge the oppressive forces exerted upon the native people of the Caribbean, but because they were decimated so early in the colonizing effort, my primary points of reference when I conceive of the colonization of the Caribbean are the Africans and Asians brought to the Caribbean as both slaves and indentured workers.

10. bell hooks, *Black Looks: Race and Representation* (Boston: South End Press, 1992), 29. See hooks for a discussion of advertisements that incorporate tropical landscapes.

11. Doris Witt, *Black Hunger: Food and the Politics of U.S. Identity* (New York: Oxford University Press, 1999), 26.

12. Witt, *Black Hunger*, 22.

13. Marianne Anthe, "'Black Names' Get Snub in Job Study," *MSNBC*. BET .com. Accessed July 29, 2003, <http://stacks.msnbc.com/news/859373.asp?cp1=1#BODY>. Path: News; Race in America. See Anthe's article for a discussion of a study completed by college professors who concentrate on concerns related to the labor market. This study was carried out over a one year period and entailed sending 5,000 qualified resumes to positions for 1,300 jobs. Those resumes with names popularly used among African Americans were more likely to be rejected than "white-named" applications. Quite interestingly, the discrimination was evident among black women's names and not among black men's. Aisha, Keisha, and Tamika ranked among the least favorable names for black women applicants.

14. E. A. Hastings, *A Glimpse of the Tropics* (London: Sampson Low, Marston & Company, Ltd, 1900).

15. Glory Robertson, "Pictorial Sources for Nineteenth-Century Women's History: Dress as a Mirror of Attitudes to Women," *Engendering History: Caribbean Women in Historical Perspective*, eds. Verene Shepherd, Bridget Brereton and Barbara Bailey (Kingston: Ian Randle Publishers, 1995), 111–22.

16. Robertson, "Pictorial Sources for Nineteenth-Century Women's History," 112.

17. For further discussion of the role of black women, see what has become known as "The Moynihan Report." Written by Daniel Moynihan and published in 1965, this report, titled *The Negro Family: The Case for National Action*, proposes the existence of a dominant black matriarchy.

18. Rosalyn Diprose, *The Bodies of Women: Ethics Embodiment and Sexual Difference* (London: Routledge, 1994).

19. Robyn Wiegman, *American Anatomies* (Durham, N.C.: Duke University Press, 1996), 48. See Wiegman for a further discussion of these ideas.

20. This scene is laden with homoerotic underpinnings, perhaps suggesting Lady's subconscious desire to assume the masculine posture of her husband and seek fulfillment across racial boundaries.

21. "Settlement Reached Regarding *The Wind Done Gone*," *Information About Suntrust v. Houghton Mifflin Company*, May 9, 2002, Houghton Mifflin, accessed July 16, 2003, <http://houghtonmifflinbooks.com/features/randall_url/statement.shtml>. Path: "Settlement Reached."

22. "Houghton Mifflin Files Appeal Brief Arguing *The Wind Done Gone* Is Fair Use of *GWTW*," *Information About Suntrust v. Houghton Mifflin Company*, May 7, 2002, Houghton Mifflin, accessed July 16, 2003, <http://houghtonmifflinbooks.com/features/randall_url/statement.shtml>. Path: "Houghton Mifflin Files Appeal."

23. "*The Wind Done Gone*: Questions and Answers About the Dispute," *Information About Suntrust v. Houghton Mifflin Company*, Houghton Mifflin, accessed July 29, 2003, <http://houghtonmifflinbooks.com/features/randall_url/qandas.shtml>.

24. "Settlement Reached Regarding the *The Wind Done Gone*."

25. "Settlement Reached Regarding the *The Wind Done Gone*."

26. See my discussion earlier in this chapter of E. A. Hastings' comments on the humor he found in seeing black, Jamaican women dressed in European fashion. Hastings' discomfort is not unlike that felt by the Mitchell Trust that wants to maintain exclusive rights to defining white (and inevitably black) identity. Interestingly both Hastings and the Mitchell Trust evoke humor in the face of uncomfortable identity territorial slippage.

27. "Toni Morrison and Major Literary Associations Join Leading Authors and Scholars in Opposition to Mitchell Trusts' Efforts to Prevent Book Publication," *Information About Suntrust v. Houghton Mifflin Company*, April 16, 2002, Houghton Mifflin, accessed July 16, 2003, <http://houghtonmifflinbooks.com/features/randall_url/statement.shtml>. Path: "Toni Morrison." As the lawsuit unfolded, Randall's novel gained national support among organizations and a range of scholars including Toni Morrison, who issued the following statement: "Considering the First Amendment rights properly accorded *Gone With the Wind*, in spite of the pain, humiliation, and outrage its ahistorical representation has caused African Americans, it seems particularly odd for the Mitchell estate to deny this clever but gentle effort to assuage the damage *Gone With the Wind* has caused. That it has asked legal redress does not seem to have embarrassed it [and] [t]o crush the artistic rights of an African American writer seems to me not only reckless but arrogant and pathetic."

28. In *Nervous Conditions*, Dangarembga intricately links Nyasha's desire for a slender body to that portion of her identity situated in a European world view. In his epic poem "Song of Lawino," Ugandan poet Okot p'Bitek makes a similar move by extending this metaphor of slenderness and directly equating it to whiteness. See Okot p'Bitek, *Song of Lawino and Song of Ocol* (London: Heinemann, 1984).

29. Paul H. Lorenz, "Anorexia and the Experience of Colonization in Tsitsi Dangarembga's *Nervous Conditions*," *The Philological Review* 23, no. 2 (1997): 41–51.

30. Sue Vice, "The Well-Rounded Anorexic Text," *American Bodies: Cultural Histories of the* Physique, ed. Tim Armstrong (New York: New York University Press, 1996), 196–203. For a discussion of the relationship between eating disorders and writing, see Vice's essay that addresses the question of whether there is "any link to be made between the various kinds of control (or loss of it) which characterize anorexia, bulimia and compulsive eating, and that which informs the act of writing" (196).

31. Hershini Bana, "The Political Economy of Food," *Proteus* 17, no. 1 (Spring 2000): 18–24. Bana further suggests that Nyasha's resistance to eating has multiple implications for her relationship with her parents, "her growing thinness contests her parents' claims of prosperity in a society, where scarcity of food and its accompanying weight loss, speaks of poverty—a suggestion Nyasha knows humiliates her father" (21).

32. Lorenz, "Anorexia and the Experience of Colonization," 47.

33. Similarly, Tambu chooses to ignore the inconsistencies and oppressive tenets of African patriarchal culture as she surges after her academic objectives, anchoring her identity in her most apparent role: "I took refuge in the image of the grateful poor female relative. That made everything a lot easier. It mapped clearly the ways I could or could not go, and by keeping within those boundaries I was able to avoid the mazes of self-confrontation" (116).

34. Literary scholar Dr. Hershini Bhana, who has herself struggled with eating disorders, explains, "Dangarembga develops the discursive replacement and metaphoric equivalency of education and food throughout *Nervous Conditions*." She further explains that "Tambu's father Jeremiah equates the consumption of knowledge/Western learning with eating. He exclaims when his brother Babmukuru returns from England, 'Our father and benefactor has returned appeased, having devoured English letters with a ferocious appetite! Did you think degrees were indigestible? If so, look at my brother. He has digested them.'"

35. The candy also serves the same purpose as the men in her life, and in Verona's relationship with Guy, she conflates him and her "sweets." There is no strong emotional connection between them, but Guy is an important source for her indulgence, and his willingness to buy candy for Verona seems to be their only interaction that pleases her (74).

36. A similar disruption occurs while Verona is dating Guy: "Normally she would pretend Guy was one of the heroes in her novels and she was an innocent blonde-haired virgin. She would walk along feeling special, then she would catch a glimpse of their reflection in a shop window and depression would descend. It would be such a shock—the fat black woman looking squat and untidy, and the old leathery-skinned white man" (74).

37. Rosalyn Diprose explains that excessively female bodies, such as those that are pregnant, menstrual or menopausal, cannot easily fit into the body politic (63).

2

The Anatomy of Sexual Unruliness

In the early nineteenth century, an important figure emerged in the arena of race-politics and imperialist conquest. Her name was Saartjie Baartman, a young South African woman who became known as the Hottentot Venus, and in contrast to the black beauty queens discussed in the introduction, Baartman's black physiology was not ideologically erased, but unrestrainedly foregrounded as the center of her identity. Her fat body, especially her buttocks, juxtaposed with her blackness has rendered Baartman one of the most frequently cited nineteenth-century icons of sexuality. This chapter explores cultural representations of sexuality among black women with fat bodies like that of Baartman and is anchored in revisionist readings of Grace Nichols' *The Fat Black Woman's Poems*, Anthony Winkler's *The Duppy* and Audre Lorde's *Zami*. Additionally, this chapter focuses on the nexus between gendered behavioral assumptions relating to both fatness and blackness with regard to sexuality. Whereas chapter one establishes the constraining boundaries of fatness and blackness in contemporary Western beauty culture, this chapter proposes that the large female body evokes sensuality, and when this body is black, it becomes a potent marker of hypersexuality as was the case with the Hottentot Venus.

Baartman was most likely an indentured servant, and in 1810 when she was twenty years old, she was taken by her employer from Cape Town to England for what became a life full of sexual exploitation.[1] Once in London, she was exhibited at Piccadilly with great financial success, and for the remainder of her short life, she was put on display across Europe.[2] Often naked and caged, a condition that implied an animalistic nature, she was whipped and forced to dance as entertainment for a white audience's licentious sense of humor.[3]

It was the postcolonial angst resulting from this oppressive legacy that literary scholar Myriam Chancy hoped to ease when she made a long-anticipated visit to France.[4] But contrary to her expectations, the trip further exposed the marginalization and objectification of black women in the postcolonial world. Chancy visited the Musée de l'Homme in Paris where she saw Saartjie Baartman's remains on display. However, Chancy did not see a mummified body or even a skeleton; rather, what she saw were Baartman's genitalia and buttocks, entombed in a display case since Baartman's death in the early eighteen hundreds. The choice to display Baartman's genitalia and buttocks was influenced by Europe's gendered and racialized perception of sexuality. Furthermore, the public visibility of the buttocks in the human anatomy make them arguably the most potent cultural signifiers of black female sexuality.[5] Chancy's postcolonial recovery was derailed by her experience because underlying the museum's display was the hegemonic perception of black women as amounting simply to the sum of their sexuality.

Baartman's abusive history and post-mortem exploitation provide an apt segue into Europe's fascination with the black female body. Her physique was a classic example of steatopygia. This feature, along with her black skin, was in contrast to Europe's vision of beauty. Specifically, there was a great deal of interest in Baartman's genitalia since she had what became known as the "Hottentot apron": unusually formed labia that Sander Gilman describes as "a hypertrophy of the labia and nymphae caused by a manipulation of the genitalia and serving as a sign of beauty among certain tribes."[6] Numerous nineteenth-century European scientists studied black women's genitalia, and Gilman suggests that this obsession with black female sexuality emerged as a component of Europe's efforts to deem black women subhuman.[7]

> [A] paradigm was needed which would technically place both the sexuality and the beauty of the black in an antithetical position to that of the white. This paradigm would have to be rooted in some type of unique and observable physical difference; they found that difference in the distinction they drew between the pathological and the normal in the medical model. (231)

Undoubtedly, Europe's reductive inclination to identify the black woman as the sum of her sexuality was also a means of justifying the rampant sexual exploitation of African women during and after slavery.

Gilman further explains that this exploitation also persisted in European art where black women's bodies functioned as an encoded sexual signifier: "[O]ne of the black servant's central functions in the visual arts of the eighteenth and nineteenth centuries was to sexualize the society in which he or she is found" (Gilman 228). This artistic use of black women to embody carnal desire in addition to Baartman's mistreatment indicates how the perception of hypersexuality as a connotation of both blackness and fatness coalesced to help concretize the marginalization of black women.[8]

Although almost two hundred years have passed since Baartman's exhibition, black women continue to inhabit a space largely defined by its hypersexuality. Cinematic representations of black women super-inscribe their sexuality, even in movies where they are not the central character. One example is the 1995 film version of *The Scarlet Letter*, directed by Roland Joffe and based on Nathaniel Hawthorne's novel of the same name. The movie's main character is Hester, a woman who engages in an adulterous affair that results in her being ostracized by her small town. This film adaptation includes highly eroticized scenes, and on each of the two occasions when Hester appears nude, images of her black servant, Mituba, are blended into the scene, blurring and displacing Hester's sexuality and instead highlighting Mituba as an eroticized object.[9]

In her essay "Selling Hot Pussy: Representations of Black Female Sexuality in the Cultural Marketplace," bell hooks discusses the eroticization of black women, particularly performers, and she suggests that their sexuality is a dominant constituent of their public profile. Hooks argues that "the black female body gains attention only when it is synonymous with accessibility, availability, when it is sexually deviant" (117). More specifically she discusses Josephine Baker, whose erotic dance routines emphasized her buttocks.[10] Hooks maintains that this emphasis was a method for taking advantage of white assumptions regarding black, female sexuality.[11] Furthermore, she interprets Diana Ross' long, frizzy hairstyle as expressing an affinity with "wildness," underscoring again an affinity between the wild and black female sexuality.[12] Hooks also mentions Tina Turner, whose stage persona is anchored in images her ex-husband Ike encountered in a 1940s movie featuring a white, female "jungle goddess" equivalent of Tarzan.[13] The irony here is that those images of the Anglo jungle-queen are based on white projections of black female sexuality, and in order to render a white woman as a sexual vessel, she was placed in an environment coded as black.

This fetishization of blackness and the black female body is a means of further installing blackness as anomalous and disorderly. As a metonym for the primal, the erotic, and the exotic, the black woman's body has been fetishized to signal sexual abandon and easy access, which situates her as the antithesis of an idealized white femininity. But race is not the only cultural target for fetishization; Western society has also created parallel cultural constructions of fatness, investing the fat body with similarly anomalous signification.

Fatness in black women is a physiological feature that functions much like the jungle setting in a Tarzan movie or as Diana Ross' untamable hair—as an encoding of sexuality and arguably blackness. Superimposing fat onto the black female body doubles its representative status as the antithesis of white femininity, since the dominant perspective on fatness in Western culture replicates the view of what blackness is already understood as denoting: bodily indiscipline and rebellion.[14] This assessment of fatness and blackness as highly sexualized concomitantly supports a Western patriarchal ideal of chastity and restraint as behavioral demonstrations of beauty. Within the parameters of Western hegemonic culture, black and fat women are incapable of sexual modesty because their very bodies, sexually active or not, are poignant sexual signifiers, permanently situating the women who bear these features as sexually uninhibited, lacking sexual/bodily control and uncontrollable.

Various cultural assumptions regarding "fat behavior" sustain this interpretation, but one of the popular media images is that of the fat woman as eternally hungry, possessing a voracious appetite. This supposed inability to ever achieve satiety implies that fat women have an unquenchable sexual appetite, and as a result, the fat female body has become fetishized as a cultural marker for carnal desire. While Freud initiated the concept of fetishism in reference to "unfit" substitutions for "the normal sexual aim," this project extends Freud's ideas with applications to the fat female body (566).[15] The West's Judeo-Christian legacy of sexual containment has created an unnatural absence of opportunities to recognize these basic yearnings, which in turn have been safely transferred to bodies that are amplified signifiers of carnal desire. As a result, the fat female body has come to represent the physiological expression of various scenes of bodily transgression and a living juxtaposition of the fulfillment of longing for both food and sex.

This and other cultural imaginings about female fleshiness result in the positioning of the fat female body in simultaneously opposing sexual spaces: first as the object of derision for that body's inability or unwillingness to conform to imperatives of slenderness and second as a site of intense desire—that body's own desire and the sexual desirability that it represents.[16] Additionally, the fat woman's excessive corporeality imbues her with an aura of masculinity, and this superimposition of masculinity on the fleshy woman also carries with it the connotation of sexual audacity.

The iconographic status of the large female body was not lost on nineteenth-century researchers, and their preoccupation with using physiological traits as an epistemology for behavioral assumptions extended to their forays into female sexuality. Several researchers sought to explain female concupiscence through quantifiable physical characteristics, and one quality that they often indicated as concurrent with promiscuity was female fatness. Gilman notes that one researcher who documented white Parisian prostitutes in the early nineteenth century described them as having a "peculiar plumpness," which was partially attributed to these women's leisurely lifestyle (Gilman 242). A separate study done by a Russian doctor also proclaims fatness as a dominant trait among the Russian prostitutes observed in a study.[17] An array of cultural circumstances may explain this phenomenon, including the greater economic independence of prostitutes. Additionally, the size boundaries for beauty were undoubtedly much less restrictive than today, and perhaps the prostitute's fleshy body was no more than a marketing tool. Whatever the case, this perception of fat as analogous to promiscuity has persisted in Western culture, and when the physical characteristics of fatness and blackness are conjoined, they create a potent cultural signifier laced with sexual overtones.

An example of such a merger between body size and race takes place in the movie *Crossing Delancey* directed by Joan Micklin Silver. In one scene a young Jewish woman displaces her sexual apprehensions upon a large black woman who functions much like the sexually encoded black servant in eighteenth-century European art.[18] The Jewish woman, Izzy, is in a sauna at her gym, and among the other occupants is a large black woman dressed in a revealing swimsuit that exposes her fleshy body as a foreshadowing of the scenes highly sexualized content.[19] In the movie, the black woman functions as a speculum of Izzy's inner sexual angst, as she discusses the explicit details of a steamy sexual encounter while Izzy listens quietly, relieved of having to display and recognize the sexual drama playing out in her own life.[20] Tania Modleski suggests that the black woman's function "is to enable the white Jewish subculture, through its heterosexual love story, to represent itself in a highly sentimentalized, romanticized, and sublimated light, while disavowing the desires and discontents underlying the civilization it is promoting" (222). This superficial performance of chastity results in the presumption that white female sexuality is a controlled and contained phenomenon, a presumption that renders both blackness and fatness as sexual outlaws, immersed in undertones of unruliness and rebellion.

Television representations of fat women also mark them as sexually unruly, often mocking their presumably elevated sexual desire by having their romantic quests perpetually thwarted by indifferent love interests. Full-figured comedian Mo'Nique stars in the UPN comedy series *The Parkers,* in which she plays the role of Miss Nikki Parker, a black, single mother who is a student at the same community college as her teenaged daughter. For the entire series Miss Parker has been in hot pursuit of one of her teachers, the suave Professor Oglevee, and in just about every episode, Professor Oglevee indelicately reminds her that she is a complete nuisance to him and deluded if she has any aspirations to become his wife. Although Miss Parker's infatuation with the professor may not have been intended as a central feature of the series when it first began, it has certainly become the most recurrent storyline in the show, and Miss Parker's unfulfilled desire is milked for every comedic moment it can provide.

These relationship dynamics between the fat, desperate woman and her dispassionate love interest are pervasive and familiar in Western culture; even children are given early exposure to the scenario. Similar circumstances unfold between the characters Miss Piggy and Kermit the Frog in the television series *The Muppet Show*. In episode after episode Miss Piggy relentlessly pursues Kermit, the object of her affection, despite his efforts to elude her, and as with Miss Parker, her unfulfilled desires are constructed as an infinite source of humor. Both Miss Parker and Miss Piggy ignore Western dictates of femininity embodied by notions of control and restriction, and they are unable to "capture" the man of their dreams.[21] Their fat bodies are tropes for their lustful sexual appetite, and their proclivity to overeat underlies a greater evil: their unruliness regarding inherited patriarchal regulations. Hence their overeating is metaphorically controlled by the rationing of their access to sex, a restriction that concretizes the representational status of the two behaviors as interchangeable.

Miss Parker and Miss Piggy both suffer from delusions that they are in mutually agreeable relationships with their love interests while the audience and the other fictional TV characters know that this is untrue. Miss Parker and Miss Piggy's inability to *see* in the way that virtually everyone else *sees* underscores the representational value of their anomalous bodies and suggests that any bodily/behavioral diversion from the culturally normative has a physical/social defect as its source. The conflict these characters experience between the real and the fictitious underlies contradictions in our responses to them and their appearance.

Both Miss Parker and Miss Piggy are wardrobe divas. They are always well dressed in highly feminized attire and ample makeup—simultaneously attractive and revolting. Their highly feminized personas are so powerful that they are both inscribed as feminine signifiers beyond the boundary of their abstract worlds, and they are both immensely popular and successful celebrities. *The Parkers* debuted in 1999, and after only its first season, the show ranked first among black households across the United States.[22] Mo'Nique Imes, who plays Miss Parker, has her own line of full-figured clothing called BBLI (Big, Beautiful and Loving It), she headlined in the successful comedy tour *Queens of Comedy*, and in 2005 she hosted Mo'Nique's Fat Chance, a full-figured women's beauty pageant. *The Muppet Show* also had widespread appeal as one of the most popular syndicated series, with a whopping audience of 235 million viewers.[23] In 1998 Miss Piggy launched her own perfume line called Moi; additionally, she has participated in ad campaigns for Baked Lays potato chips and Denny's restaurants.[24] Angela Stukator suggests that Miss Piggy is a particularly unstable character: "From a feminist perspective we might examine Miss Piggy as an unruly woman who acquires oppositional power from her ambivalence: she is the object of disgust and desire, being both repellent and attractive, strong and delicate, friendly and hostile, and most significantly, woman and animal" (197).[25] Miss Piggy's nonhuman status is an appropriate symbol of the deviance associated with the fat female body, a form of deviance that implies Miss Piggy and other fat women are partially unnatural, animalistic divergences.

The female body has long occupied this lawless territory, its anatomical difference from the masculine normative marking it as an aberration. This perception is arguably rooted in Aristotle's *The Generation of Animals*, where he suggests that the male body operates as a biological norm and the female body as a variation: "[W]e should look upon the female state as being as it were a deformity, though one which occurs in the ordinary course of nature" (461).[26] The transformative ability inherent in the female body's reproductive capacity reinforces that body's freakishness because of its capacity to radically transform itself. Furthermore, because the female body defies the principle of a "fixed" physiological state of being, it is often construed as monstrous.[27] This presumption of biological disorder associated with the female body is echoed by assumptions of disorderly behavior. Dominant among these assumptions are those myths related to personality changes concurrent with hormonal fluctuations during such biological events as pregnancy or the pre-menstrual stage. Comedians abound with jokes regarding the "monstrous" behavior of women at these points of hormonal flux, and the implication of hysteria as endemic to femininity suggests that this condition of monstrosity is latent at all times.[28]

The fifteenth-century document *The Malleus Maleficarum*, written within this perceptual context of women as monsters, was published to aid in the identification and trial of individuals practicing witchcraft.[29] During this time the text was in prolific use, and a copy purportedly "lay on the bench of every judge, on the desk of every magistrate. It was the ultimate, irrefutable, unarguable authority. It was implicitly accepted not only by Catholic but Protestant legislature" (viii).[30] *The Malleus* assists in the stigmatization of women as unnatural freaks by situating a range of perceived behavioral differences in their anatomy. In part one, question six of *The Malleus*, a section that seeks to explain why women are more prone to involvement in the supernatural, the text explains that a woman "is more carnal than a man, as is clear from her many carnal abominations. And it should be noted that there was a defect in the formation of the first woman, since she was formed from a bent rib. . . . And since through this defect she is an imperfect animal, she always deceives" (44). *The Malleus* adds further detail, explaining that "just as through the first defect in their intelligence they are more prone to abjure the faith; so through their second defect of inordinate affections and passions they search for, brood over, and inflict various vengeances, either by witchcraft, or by some other means" (45). The function of these readings of the female body and female behavior as abnormal extends beyond *The Malleus'* intended use of persecuting women who were disruptive to patriarchal hegemony. Moreover, these readings constitute one arm of a syncretic mechanism that combines misogynistic religious and philosophical beliefs and contributes to the marginalization of women in Western discourse and culture.

One of the strategic benefits to patriarchal discourse in rendering women's bodies and behavior anomalous is that this act restricts participation in the body politic, conceived of as both white and male. Robyn Wiegman suggests that white masculinity is "the universal condition of political entitlement," and that those whose bodies differ are distanced from the seat of political control dependent on the extent of their bodily variation from both whiteness and maleness (49). Women who seek to assert themselves, whether in the public or private sphere, are often strategically animalized and referred to by terms such as "bitch" and "vixen" in an effort to further concretize them as monstrosities, exacerbating the pre-existent cultural conception of them as a biological departure from the normative.[31] The fat woman's body then becomes even more susceptible to this rationale since its excessive flesh and its corporeal dominance implies its monstrosity. Furthermore, as I mentioned previously, the fat woman evokes an essence of masculinity, and it is perhaps a fear of the political implications such a transformation suggests that has contributed to the fat female body's rejection and marginalization.

As a result of this gynophobia, one of the patriarchy's impulses has been to institute bodily control over women, juxtaposing various constructions of race, beauty, and gender to craft an ideal image of womanhood. The creation of this feminine archetype effectively diminishes women's power by enhancing the likelihood that the female body will diverge from the culturally normative, which legitimates hegemonic interventions in the corporeal autonomy of those with deviant physiologies. Hazel Carby explains that under the guise of maintaining moral propriety, the bodies of black women in urban post-slavery settings were "policed" by both white and black institutions.[32] By implying impending moral degeneracy, an article written in 1905 recommends various tactics including the creation of "a controlled system of lodging houses where black women can be sent at night and kept from going off on their own into the streets" (Carby 24). This evocation of black women as both predatory and animalistic, unable to exert bodily/sexual control, is echoed in modern propaganda regarding fatness.

The media is rife with invitations to reinstate bodily restraint, and a plethora of advertisements encourage women to regain control of their bodies. Le'a Kent suggests that in the public sphere fatness must not only be controlled but utterly demolished for one's life to function with any semblance of equilibrium: "[F]at bodies, and fat women's bodies in particular, are represented as a kind of abject: that which must be expelled to make all other bodily representations and functions, even life itself, possible" (135).[33] This sentiment is echoed in numerous testimonial ads for weight-loss products that mostly feature women expounding upon the meaninglessness of their lives prior to their shedding of some pounds.

It is this construction of fatness as repulsive and deserving only of erasure that Maya Angelou teases in her poem "Phenomenal Woman."[34] The poem's protagonist opens by establishing herself as a large woman who is beyond the boundaries of traditional Euro-feminine beauty norms (130). This full-figured narrator then proceeds with a glorified liturgy of her physical attributes that mark her as an exceptional and intriguing woman despite her otherness. Angelou explains that she wrote "Phenomenal Woman" for large women, "for those who don't like their size but will do little about it except call a friend," as well as for "fat women who love their bodies, who know they are the epitome of sensuality and when they walk down the street no one, male or female, can keep their eyes off them" (Angelou qtd. in Cunningham).[35] Angelou adds that she also "wrote it for skinny women, those who deserve our sympathy" (Angelou qtd. in Cunningham). Angelou's juxtaposition of fatness and exceptionality infuses that body's uniqueness with sensuality and the suggestion of expansive strength. Her sly comment about slender women implies that their adherence to traditional beauty standards creates the experience of loss.

Grace Nichols also employs representations of the fat black woman in her collection *The Fat Black Woman's Poems*. By creating a protagonist whose otherness is triply configured through her race, gender, and size, Nichols contests the marginalization of non-white and non-male individuals within a Caribbean postcolonial context. The resistance to controlling impulses exerted over both black women and fat women fuels Nichols' glorification of the fat black woman in a tacit rejection of Western beauty norms and constructions of race.

Nichols' collection situates the fat black woman's sexuality and her self-perceived sensuality as central to her resistance to hegemonic forces. In the poem "Invitation," the fat black woman addresses potential suitors, proudly offering detailed descriptions of her fat body. Her large, ungraspable breasts and her slippery thighs suggest the elusiveness of her sexuality, a result of her immense body and subsequently a bodily representation of sexual and cultural independence (13). Additionally, the fat black woman is quite comfortable and secure with her body, and expresses her resistance to imperatives of slenderness (12).

In another poem titled "Thoughts Drifting Through the Fat Black Woman's Head While Having a Full Bubble Bath," the fat black woman situates her body and its largeness as analogous to various elements of her natural environment. She uses the term "steatopygous" to describe herself as well as these natural occurrences, validating her body as an acceptable physiology to inhabit and not a deviant anomaly (15).[36] She also expresses her rejection of Western epistemology since it names fatness as an abnormality (15). This poem impoes an inverse relationship between honoring the black, female body and the status of Eurocentric epistemological practices. According to Alison Easton, "a celebration of the female body will not be possible without first consciously and directly subverting the white traditions of signification and those narratives they call history."[37] Furthermore, this poem suggests that the fat black woman's sexuality, embodied by her breasts, is vital anti-colonial ammunition against history's misrepresentations, its vacuums and its painful legacy for people of color. Jana Evans Braziel explains that "fat female bodies undermine the stability of western metaphysical and dualistic thought: they topple philosophical binarisms in which the female is subordinated to the male, the body subordinated to the soul, and materiality to form" (232). The poem's title helps to situate the fat black woman's destabilizing prowess as grounded in her self-acceptance and ability to take pleasure in her expansive body, since it is while enjoying a bubble bath that she generates these thoughts.

The fat black woman is also engaged in an act of reclamation, and the unruliness of her immense body concomitantly echoes the unruly speech in her poems. "The Fat Black Woman Goes Shopping" features our protagonist roaming London in search of comfortable clothing. In this poem the hegemony's chilling oppression is symbolized as the bitter winter cold through which she must navigate in search of properly fitting clothes while the slender white mannequins seem to laugh at her (11). The unaccommodating weather of the British metropole as well as its sparse fashion choices signal a firm grasp of her colonial legacy. The combination of the skinny wax models with this intemperate geographic as well as cultural milieu coalesces to combine colonial imperialism and the "tyranny of slenderness."[38]

In response to this pressure to conform to hegemonic beauty dictates, the fat black woman rebels with her tongue and commences with a proverbial Caribbean "tongue lashing" as she curses in African languages and Caribbean patois (11). As the fat black woman bemoans the extensive walking she must do in search of suitable clothes, she simultaneously invokes the long voyage of the Middle Passage as the source of her anguish. Images of physical coercion and emaciated bodies evoked by the Middle Passage are in contrast to the image of the fat black woman. In her verbal retaliation she abandons her English "mother tongue," choosing instead African languages that function beyond the colonial constraints of English. The fat black woman's quest for an appropriate medium to voice her anguish mirrors Nichols' own concerns as a writer. Nichols explains that she is enticed by the opportunities to "battle with language" that writing poetry provides, and she describes her creative efforts as "the challenge of trying to create or chisel out a new language" (284).[39]

One feature of the fat black woman's language is its promiscuity—an extension of the sexuality she embodies. In a discussion of how women inhabit the physical space around them, Sandra Lee Bartky suggests that their reluctance to locate their physical bodies beyond the boundaries of an imagined restrictive corral is violated by the behavior of loose or sexually deviant women.[40] Bartky contends, "Her looseness is manifest not only in her morals, but in her manner of speech, and quite literally in the free and easy way she moves," suggesting that sexual agility and verbal agility are coterminous and exist in a similar ideological space that is free from patriarchal control (134). Such is the case for the fat black woman whose curses and fleshy body disrupt Western expectations of femininity.

Grace Nichols is usefully compared with Anthony Winkler, a contemporary white-identified Jamaican living in the U.S.A., who is author of *The Duppy*, a novel that also disrupts a Westernized vision of womanhood and engages representations of the "loose" woman, specifically a shopkeeper named Miss B, whose highly sexualized, large black body becomes one of the primary sites where racial, cultural and socioeconomic anxieties play out in the novel. Moreover, Miss B's uninhibited embrace of her sexuality is a metaphor for her resistance to neocolonialist oppression. This novel, narrated in the first person, begins with the death of a frugal and contentious Jamaican shopkeeper, Mr. Taddeus Baps. This Scrooge-like character is busy pouring over his accounts early one morning when he dies from a massive heart attack and turns into a duppy.[41] To Baps' surprise there is no white light, no tunnel and no angelic host to sweep him away in a fiery chariot. Instead, his celestial guide is Hopeton, a local thief who was shot some years prior during a burglary, and Baps' journey to heaven begins on a crowded Jamaican minibus and culminates in a cane field where he must crawl through a drainpipe that leads to the promised land. After a great deal of protest over the indignity of his post-mortem circumstances, Baps decides to enter the suspect culvert, and it does in fact transport him to heaven—Jamaican heaven.

The Duppy

Along with his guide, Baps materializes at the other end of the drainpipe to find that the landscape and people of Jamaican heaven are much like those of the Jamaica he has left behind on Earth, and among other things, there is government bureaucracy. Baps must get registered in "the official government book of arriving souls," so he and Hopeton journey through the picturesque countryside to a grocery shop operated by Miss B, who is also the local registrar (43–44). This journey marks the start of Baps' ideological journey and *The Duppy*'s contestation of Western economic and cultural practices by questioning socioeconomic policy, religion, beauty ideals, and heterosexual politics. This ideological challenge is facilitated by Miss B's fat persona, one of the sites where this contestation is most pronounced, but it is initiated by the various paradigmatic shifts that heaven represents.

Despite the cosmetic similarities between heaven and Earth, there are some essential differences regarding an individual's relationship with his or her material body. First, people do not have belly buttons until they are about to reincarnate on Earth (38). This absence signals a disconnection of the body from its physical origins, reorienting heaven's inhabitants as spiritual beings. Furthermore, physical pain is experienced as a form of intense physical pleasure. Baps makes this discovery when he first arrives and is clouted over the head by a jealous wife who mistakes him for the philandering husband she left behind (32–33). "You stinking brute, you! You finally reach!" the woman screams as she pummels Baps with a rock (33). And although the blow is severe enough that Baps falls on the ground, to his surprise the clout is an extremely pleasurable experience for him (33, 36). "'What a way dat rockstone lick sweet,'" Baps exclaims; Hopeton acknowledges Baps' pleasure, adding "Wait till a madman chop off you head with a machete! Now if you want something sweet, dat really sweet" (36). Throughout *The Duppy* as Baps and others are assaulted and maimed, they revel in the pleasure of the experience, marking a triumph of their divine bodies over the tribulations of the flesh they might have experienced on Earth. Many of these potential tribulations, such as overexposure to violence, limited access to appropriate housing and nutrition, and poor health care are associated with disadvantageous social circumstances that result from the Caribbean's colonial legacy.

This notion of physiological conquest is further engaged within the context of sexuality, and all new arrivals to Jamaican heaven must complete a form accepting or rejecting sexual neutering. This form, designed for conservative Christians who cannot reconcile the idea of heaven with sexual activity, allows for the "painless" removal of the penis or the sealing of the vagina by someone "licensed" with the heavenly Jamaican government to perform such services (45). Baps promptly refuses this offer (45). The provision of this castrating alternative mocks traditional Judeo-

Christian conservatism regarding sexual intercourse by suggesting that sexual disinterest is not a divine requirement but actually an unnatural choice.

The Duppy also contests traditional Western notions of beauty, and Baps is a dedicated adherent to the perception that female fatness is unattractive. When Miss B makes sexual advances towards him, Baps retorts: "Fatty woman don't turn me on!" (49). Miss B persists in her seductive efforts, stating, "Dis is heaven. Every woman turn on every man. All woman have to do is jump on and the table spread and ready" (49). Miss B's explanation asserts that the marginalization of her fat, unruly body is not specific to that body but to the pervading social context within which that body is perceived. She elaborates along this strain in another conversation with Baps:

> One day the subject of Miss B's big belly came up, and I asked her bluntly why she continued to resemble a breeding Red Poll cow when she could just as easily look like better, but she growled that she happened to love herself black and fat, which was why she hadn't availed herself either of government bleaching or thinning. She boastfully declared that she liked being beefy, loved her jelly belly, and was perfectly content to perch on her stool and float on a tube of batty fat. (53)

Miss B's comments implicate the third world political machinery as a conduit for Westernized visions of beauty that peripheralize the large black female body, since it is the heavenly Jamaican government that provides the services which would allow Miss B to transform herself into a closer approximation of white femininity by becoming more slender and light-skinned. It is Miss B's unwillingness to make use of this transformative opportunity that baffles Baps; however, the pleasurable sexual relationship that develops between them undermines his ambivalence towards her appearance and suggests that the perception of beauty does not correlate to the potential for sexual pleasure as Baps and Western beauty politics might assume. He eventually recognizes the fulfillment of his physical and emotional relationship with Miss B as unparalleled when he states, "During these happy times, no man in heaven was happier or slept sweeter than I, Taddeus Baps" (56).

Despite this eventually fulfilling outcome of Baps' affair with Miss B, the relationship does not begin on mutually agreeable terms, but rather out of Baps' need for a place to stay. After he completes his arrival paperwork, he realizes that unlike his earthly life that was full of responsibilities, he now has nothing to do. Having been a shopkeeper, he decides to hang around Miss B's to help out in her grocery store, and later that night he retires to a bedroom adjoining the shop. He falls into a deep sleep only to wake up shortly after and find Miss B naked on top of him, primed for sexual intercourse. At first he resists, but Miss B is not discouraged by his rejection, and eventually Baps acquiesces to her demands for sex: "[S]he was humping up a jamboree and her wiggling and jiggling was so powerful that I soon found myself clinging to beefy batty for dear life until the two of us exploded simultaneously on the bed with a noisy bellowing" (49–50). Shortly after recovering from their tryst, Miss B announces that she is ready to engage in another round of sex. "You mad?" Baps asks her, "I done for de night" (50). "In heaven man don't done until woman say so," Miss B rejoins, and much to Baps' pleasure they engage in a total of twenty-five rounds of intercourse, lasting until the following morning (50–51).

In Winkler's version of heaven both men and women have extraordinary sexual stamina, a characteristic that supports the idea that sex is a divine and acceptable engagement since divine bodies are engineered to maximize the benefits of intercourse. Furthermore, Miss B's willingness to initiate the encounter, as well as her declaration that "man don't done until woman say so," legitimates female desire and reverses the traditional imbalance of power in heterosexual relationships to privilege the woman's sexual demands. Additionally, there is no shame associated with sex, and it becomes a sort of divine public ritual instead of a shameful, private sin. When a customer enters Miss B's shop on the morning of the twenty-five session marathon with Baps, without hesitation Miss B yells from the back room, informing the customer that she and Baps are having sex:

> "I grinding Baps, Cynthia. Serve youself."
>
> After a delicate hesitation from the shop, the customer answered with a mirthful cackling, "When you done, I can grind Baps, too?"
>
> "If anything left when I finish!"
>
> "Dis is heaven Miss B! You know it never use up here, even after all sisters share it. Hallelujah!"
>
> "Glory be!" Miss B blathered her agreement into my ear, heaving tirelessly. (51)

Miss B's remarks indicate that heavenly paradigms further contest Eurocentric monogamous ideals because women have the opportunity to engage in polygamous intimate arrangements.

Moreover, the cries of "Glory Be!" and "Hallelujah!" coming from Miss B and her customer echo *The Duppy*'s conflation of sexuality and the divine.[42] This commingling of sexuality and religiosity—presumably contradictory subjects based on Christian ideology—is most blatantly enacted when Miss B takes Baps to church with her. At first he protests, questioning the need to attend church now that he has arrived in heaven (54). However, she explains that acceptance into heaven is unrelated to church-going activities, which confirms Winkler's contention that Christian ideology privileges performance over inner character (54). Eventually when they both go to the local church, Miss B begins to fondle Baps' crotch in the middle of a hymn (54). He is outraged by her disregard for the sanctity of their setting, and during a whispered quarrel she argues that in heaven the entire human physiology "participated fully and equally in formal worship" (55). Baps simply cannot come to terms with such a dramatic paradigm shift, and so he compromises, allowing Miss B to fondle him if she is not holding the hymnal at the same time. Grudgingly she agrees, scolding Baps for "fostering a backward colonial mentality" (56). This accusation further confirms that Baps is a compendium of neocolonial attitudes anchored in an ideology that relegates sexuality to the margins as it does Miss B's unruly, fat body.

As a further affront to traditional notions regarding intimacy, the heavenly code of conduct reclassifies romantic relationships beyond the patriarchal context of ownership.

On occasion Miss B offers to "loan" Baps out to her friends as a thoughtful gesture: "Sometimes at the end of the day, as Miss B was locking up, she would turn and bawl over her shoulder, 'Baps, do me a favour! Run 'round to Miss Simpson and give her a good grind. When you reach back, honeybunch, you supper will be ready" (56). Miss B's willingness to disavow monogamy and traditional rites of romantic ownership and to situate Baps as communal property, speaks to the text's resistance against the structure of patriarchal romantic relationships, which feature the possessor and the possessed.

This trope of differentiation between Western capitalism and heavenly socialism also applies to heaven's economy, and Miss B's shop is a poignant signifier of alternate economic possibilities. Just as her fat body is associated with an abundance of sexuality, she is also linked to material abundance.[43] Thus, when Baps arrives at Miss B's, he is struck by her imprudent financial management. Customers can serve themselves and take food on credit as they please (47). When Miss B is later reborn on Earth and Baps takes complete control of the shop, he immediately abandons this credit policy, insisting that everyone use cash (61). He begins to restrict the quantity of products customers may purchase in order to create the appearance of scarcity and accommodate a more capitalistic economic model where corporate prowess reigns: "What was the fun of owning a shop," he asks, "if the shopkeeper wasn't in a position to make customers beg him to sell them goods?" (62). However, Baps' plan is undermined because Miss B's shop is as unruly as her large body and equivalent in its material abundance.

Baps begins his first day in charge by taking inventory (62). When he finishes, he removes a tin of sardines and eats it for his breakfast;

however, when he returns to the shelf where he got the sardines, he realizes that another tin has appeared in its place:

> No matter how many tins of sardines I took off the shelf, I always had three remaining.
>
> As I stood there marveling at this replenishment, I realized that this was why Miss B had been so careless with her stocktaking, because she never could run out of anything! (62–63)

But instead of relaxing his plans for more austere financial measures, Baps decides to take advantage of the situation for his sole benefit: "Under the circumstances—controlling the only shop in the village and having no overhead plus an endless supply of free goods—I saw at once that the only sensible business move was to drastically mark-up prices and gouge the shopping public" (63). However, a tree in Miss B's backyard begins bearing money, which allows her customers to purchase whatever they want (66).

Aside from symbolizing abundance, Miss B is also the embodiment of the type of person whom Baps often refers to as "ole negar," a derogatory Jamaican expression that conflates blackness and an absence of gentility, and within the context of the novel, Baps' use of this term indicates his ambivalence and anxiety about his own blackness and socioeconomic status. On their first encounter he describes Miss B in terms that reflect this juxtaposition of unruliness, represented by Miss B's fat body, and blackness, represented by her hair: "[I]nside, slouched behind the counter and squinting at a newspaper, was a big, fatty woman whose frizzy head was bound in a calico wrap and speckled by a swarm of flies" (42). Moreover, Miss B's shop is itself an "ole negar": "It was a perfect country shop," Baps explains, "in the sense a woman means when she calls a man a 'perfect brute'" (42). By naming Miss B's business a "country" shop, Winkler situates its rural placement and dislocation from the sophistication of the city as central to the shop and Miss B's identity. And equating the shop with a disorderly man seals its signification as the antithesis of decorum. Hence Miss B's fatness prefigures her wanton sexuality, and both qualities are embodied by the unruliness of her business, in turn rendering her a potent evocation of blackness on an economic and social plane—the two dominant arenas from which the concept of "ole negar" derives.

Throughout *The Duppy*, Baps constantly expresses his disdain for "ole negar," intimating his representative status as a neocolonial imperialist. Baps even admits to Hopeton, his celestial escort, that what he most enjoyed about his earthly life as a shopkeeper was that it allowed him to "impose discipline and fiscal restraint over ole negar" (18). Furthermore, when Miss B's tree begins bearing money, thwarting Baps' plans to overcharge customers, he complains that "again ole negar had made [him] look like monkey" (67). Baps' curious engagement with the concept of "ole negar" reaches its zenith further on in the novel after he meets God and the two become close friends. As they prepare to take a vacation together, God decides to change appearances and asks for Baps' permission to scramble about in his consciousness to find an image to assume (103). Baps enthusiastically agrees, and to his dismay, God metamorphoses into an "ole negar" because this impression in Baps' brain is so overwhelming (103).

God's transformation is a poignant rebuttal of Bap's classist and racist ideologies since God's assumption of an "ole negar" persona legitimates that identity as divine. Baps is a stalwart symbol of the Jamaican middle class and its fears of merging with the predominantly black working class. Such an amalgamation would result in the middle class becoming displaced from its economic and social approximation to whiteness. As a result, Baps forever positions himself as superior to "ole negar" to differentiate himself from this specific construction of race in an effort to exorcise his own blackness. Kim Robinson-Walcott points out that Baps' fear of "ole negar" results in a "schizophrenic self-hatred" that is masterfully revealed when Baps first dies, leaves his body, and observes himself on the floor of his living room (26).[44]

> What was this? I indignantly asked myself. Has some ole negar come and dead in my drawing room at this early hour without asking permission? I was about to kick the brute and tell him to get up and go dead on government road when I realised—to my horror—that the ole negar dead on the floor was none other than me, Taddeus Baps. (4)

This fear is in part responsible for his initial rejection of Miss B as a sexual partner because he relates her fat and unkempt appearance to an "ole negar."

Miss B's divine body also reveals the opposing dualities between a Western vision of the world and alternate ideologies. This paradigmatic conflict is anchored in contradictory cultural imaginings of heaven and Winkler resists the dominant Eurocentric perception of paradise, which he configures as a marginalization of blackness. For example, when Baps first arrives in heaven he is unable to fully appreciate his beautiful and luxuriant tropical surroundings as an authentic paradise. And as he walks through the heavenly countryside on his way to Miss B's, he finally pinpoints his discomfort: "Where de sheep?" he asks Hopeton, "You need sheep, man, if you want a true heaven!" (38–39). Baps' sense that Jamaican heaven is not genuine emerges from his assessment of whiteness as racially normative and blackness as an approximation of such. Jamaican heaven's bushy tropical landscape, while splendorous, remains an imitation of the bucolic vision of northern green pastures and grazing sheep. Similarly Miss B's fat body is incongruous with Baps' expectation of heaven: "You don't even look like an angel. Angel not supposed to be so meaty," he says to her (46). "I am not a damn angel!" she responds, explaining, "I am a Jamaican! If you want angel, you have to migrate to America and join sheep heaven" (46).

While Winkler's portrayal of the black female body in some ways resists neocolonial imperatives of slenderness, I found the carnivalesque quality of that portrayal disquieting, leading me to question how Winkler's subject position as a white Jamaican male might have affected his envisioning of Miss B's persona. Although Winkler situates Miss B as a sexual dynamo despite her large size, the narrative never contextualizes her body as an alternative but appreciable aesthetic form. Miss B's fat body is persistently unruly and persistently unattractive, and Baps' favorable reception of the sexual pleasure she provides him seems entirely disconnected from any appreciation of the body with which she performs those pleasurable acts. Furthermore, if one of Winkler's goals is to engage the black woman's body, why does the text imply that Miss B's body is so unearthly and practically unnatural in its corpulence?

As a white male, Winkler observes bodies such as those like Miss B's with a gaze that bears some parallels to that of his racial forbears—the colonizers who viewed the indigenous "other." That gaze is inevitably rooted in the distinction between "us" and "them" because it originates within the context of racial constructions, which the colonial endeavor leaves practically no space to circumvent. Winkler's status as the observer who looks from a colonially defined position of racial and gender superiority perhaps leads to his exaggeration of Miss B's otherness because he is limited in his ability to gauge the pre-existent cultural distance of her subject position from his own. In his effort to fashion a character who embodies otherness as he understands it, Miss B ends up as a caricature of a caricature—the already misimagined identity of black, Caribbean femininity.

Nevertheless, in *The Duppy*, Miss B's large, divine body is an important site for Winkler's engagement with postcolonial issues of race and class and an effective foil for Baps' neo-imperialist attitudes. According to Mary Condé, large women contest stereotypes: "Fat women in fiction derive their literary, if not their social, power from the ways in which they illuminate and challenge society's expectations about gender, race and identity" (129). Miss B's fat body and uninhibited sexuality both characterize the unruliness she is meant to represent, and this resistance to Eurocentric notions of order is concomitantly an embrace of Caribbean identity as authentic.

In Audre Lorde's "biomythography" *Zami: A New Spelling of My Name,* Lorde also refuses to accept a marginalized identity. The text chronicles Lorde's childhood and young adult years during which she negotiates her queer sexual identity as well as her cultural identity as the child of Caribbean immigrants living in Harlem. As a self-described visually challenged, fat, black lesbian, Lorde is aware of the ways in which she unsettles Western notions of femininity, but instead of resigning herself to her virtually guaranteed subject position as an outsider, she frames her life story as the transcendence of otherness. Furthermore, her large, sensuous body and her sexual adventures become motifs for rebellion and unruliness.

Lorde begins her narrative by repeatedly invoking the image of her fat mother, Linda, and by simultaneously inscribing her own Caribbean roots. As Lorde recounts experiences with her mother, she offers numerous anecdotes that portray Linda's rambunctious yet resourceful qualities, thus grounding Linda's resistance in an alternate, non-Western frame of knowledge:

> She knew about mixing oils for bruises and rashes, and about disposing of all toenail clippings and hair from the comb. About burning candles before All Souls Day to keep the soucoyants away, lest they suck the blood of her babies. She knew about blessing the food and yourself before eating, and about saying prayers before going to sleep. (10)

But as Lorde notes in the final sentence of the quote, Linda is also aware of Judeo-Christian beliefs, and her strength derives from her ability to traverse potentially opposing frames of knowledge and by extension opposing worlds.

Linda's resistance to the racism she and her family experience prefigures Lorde's sexual and political unruliness, and Lorde invokes her mother's fat body as a metaphor for Linda's assertiveness:

> My mother was a very private woman, and actually quite shy, but with a very imposing, no-nonsense exterior. Full-bosomed, proud, and of no mean size, she would launch herself down the street like a ship under full sail, usually pulling me stumbling behind her. Not too many hardy souls dared cross her prow too closely. (17)

In addition to her imposing presence, Linda practices her own brand of political and social activism. During the Second World War, a time of air-raid drills at Lorde's school, Linda participates in the school's wartime efforts by joining other mothers on the school's rooftop to look out for enemy planes (55). Furthermore, she boycotts shops whose proprietors offended her while groceries were rationed (21). Linda's temperament contributes to a rift between her and her daughter because Linda wants permanent access to her children's private life. Lorde imagines that the growing gap between her and Linda is partially related to her appearance: "[S]he didn't love me because I was bad and I was fat" (83–84). Although Lorde's conclusions may seem like childish exaggerations, she accurately recognizes the metaphorical connotation of her fat body as a signifier of disobedience. Interestingly, Lorde is quite literally her mother's child in this respect as they are both large, assertive, and unruly women.

Lorde, too, is militant in her political perspective and rebellious towards the sociopolitical establishment, but unlike her mother, Lorde expresses her disavowal of the patriarchal power structure through sexual unruliness. Lorde builds this disavowal into the framework of her narrative, and as she chronicles her life, Lorde links her sexual explorations to concurrently emergent periods of sociopolitical awareness and activism in her life. As she narrates her resistance to hegemonic control, that recitation also becomes a rejection of hegemonic heterosexual imperatives as well as a celebration of her queer sexuality.

One of Lorde's earlier homoerotic experiences takes place during her freshman year in high school when she meets another young black girl named Gennie. Regarding Gennie Lorde states: "[She] was the first person in my life that I was ever conscious of loving. She was my first true friend" (87). The relationship is never consummated, but descriptions of Lorde and Gennie's intimacy are imbued with sexual underpinnings as the two friends walk through Harlem holding hands (89) or cuddle together on Gennie's couch while it snows outside (93). However, almost as a substitute for the absence of their literal sexual disobedience, Lorde offers a transgressive narrative detailing all the boundaries she and Gennie breach: they smoke in public, skip school, steal from their mothers and seduce Latino boys (86). Then as a literal extension of the intimate transformative opportunities provided by their relationship, they also favor donning a variety of costumes and roaming New York pretending to be other than whom they are: "Bandits, Gypsies, Foreigners of all degrees, Witches, Whores and Mexican Princesses—there were appropriate costumes for every role, and appropriate places in the city to go to play them all out" (88). Lorde frames her narrative of their relationship with commentary on the sociopolitical transformations taking place around them by noting Ghandi's victory in India, China's conversion to communism, and Israel's birth as a new nation (87). More specifically she notes her own burgeoning awareness of America's racist environment when a white waitress refuses to serve ice cream to her family during a visit to the nation's capital (87).

One of Lorde's earliest sexual encounters with a woman is also framed with a neo-resistance narrative of sexual enlightenment. Lorde moves to Stamford, Connecticut, in search of a job and meets Ginger at the electronics factory where they both work. Ginger is Puerto Rican and also large like Lorde, who describes Ginger as having "a body like the Venus of Willendorf" (136). By invoking this ancient goddess image, Lorde asserts the divine nature of the fat female body in rebuttal to opposing contemporary Western notions of sexual attractiveness. Furthermore, she continues to describe Ginger by eroticizing Ginger's large body and suggesting its heightened sexual appeal: "Ginger was gorgeously fat, with an open knowledge about her body's movement that was delicate and precise. Her breasts were high and ample. She had pads of firm fat upon her thighs, and round dimpled knees" (136). In addition to finding Ginger's fat body attractive, Lorde also contradicts Judeo-Christian imperatives of sexual containment and inhibition by constructing her first sexual encounter as a divine experience, extending the religious trope introduced by her description of Ginger as the Venus of Willendorf.

Lorde portrays her initial lovemaking episode as a sort of spiritual revelation, combining what many would view as the profane with the divine in a defiant assertion of her homosexuality:

> Ginger's breath warmed my neck and started to quicken. My hands moved down over her round body, silky and fragrant, waiting. Uncertainty and doubt rolled away from the mouth of my wanting like a great stone, and my unsureness dissolved in the directing heat of my own frank and finally open desire. (139)

Lorde's metaphor of a stone being dislodged from an aperture evokes the image of Jesus' resurrection. This imagery suggests a parallel between Lorde's sexual awakening and the spiritual revolution represented by the metaphor of Christ's resurrection. On a more literal level, Lorde's imagery also suggests the initiation of sexual freedom, and specifically lesbian liberation. What Lorde refers to as "the mouth of her wanting" can quite literally be viewed as the vagina and the errant stone construed to represent similar doubts and fears as those that impeded Christ's followers from believing that he defied death.

Lorde's relationship with Ginger is contextualized by a concurrent narrative of racial enlightenment, specifically with regard to the American education system. When Lorde first arrives in Stamford, she visits the Crispus Attucks Center seeking assistance with finding a job. "Some local dignitary, no doubt," Lorde comments when she reads the name of the center, unaware of Attucks' historical legacy (124). It is only later after meeting Ginger that Lorde becomes aware of Attucks' historical significance. "Well I'll be dipped. Slick kitty from the city! What kind of school was that you-all went to?" Ginger exclaims when she realizes that Lorde has no idea that the center is named after a black man and that he was the first person to die in the American Revolution (131). This realization about the deficiencies in her education is a significant milestone for Lorde and encourages her to further contemplate the knowledge she has been denied, furthering her political awareness and activism.

She eventually returns to New York and becomes involved with the Committee to Free the Rosenbergs, who were being held on charges of espionage.[45] Lorde demonstrates and pickets on their behalf, even traveling to Washington in their support (148). Interestingly, Lorde's narrative of her renewed political militancy is intertwined with descriptions of her mounting desire to visit Mexico, a place she has mythologized as "the accessible land of color and fantasy and delight" (147). Despite the efforts of protestors, the Rosenbergs are subsequently electrocuted, and after that Lorde redirects her efforts and instead plans to visit Mexico—known during this period as a retreat for activists (149).

After Lorde finally makes it to her land of "fantasy," she meets an American woman named Eudora, and they eventually become lovers. Once again Lorde crafts her relationship as a plane of her political rebellion, her fat and sensuous body doing double time as a metaphor for both sexual and political unruliness. Like several other American expatriates residing in Mexico, Eudora has been an unruly entity herself. Lorde explains that Eudora "became the first woman to attend the University of Texas, integrating it by camping out on the university grounds for four years in a tent with her rifle and a dog" since the university administration denied her living accommodations (162). Eudora's unruliness as well as the anti-American sentiment of the expatriates residing in Mexico imbue her and Lorde's affair with her with an aura of deviance. For example, Eudora has had a mastectomy and is self-conscious about her missing breast (165). But once again Lorde rejects the traditional beauty norms that favor physiological wholeness, finding Eudora sexually attractive despite her disfigurement. Lorde signals this appreciation for Eudora's body by insisting that they make love with the lights on as opposed to in the darkness as Eudora initially prefers (168).

Like Ginger, Eudora also teaches Lorde about her African heritage, informing her about the pre-Colombian presence of Africans in the Americas evidenced by the Olmec statues that had been discovered (170). Additionally, Eudora enlightens Lorde regarding the repercussions of the European presence in the Americas. She highlights environmental issues relating to deforestation as well as the genocidal impact of Europeans on the Native Indians (170). Eudora positions the Christian church as yet another source of oppression, explaining that some Mexican women have been forced to give Catholic names to their pagan goddesses in order to avoid persecution from the church (170).[46]

Lorde's biomythography closes with her engaged in an act of divine renegotiation, similar to the renaming of pagan goddesses. She meets a woman named Afrekete, whose name unabashedly implies her association with Africa, and Lorde constructs their sexual relationship as a divine encounter laden with Afrocentric spiritual signification. Quite notably, Lorde invokes fatness as an important component of the spiritual and cultural rejuvenation Afrekete instigates, further centering the fat black, female body as a disorderly source of disruption against hegemonic sexual and racial oppression. Interestingly, Afrekete is not large; however, Lorde ascribes largeness as one of her features: "I kept thinking [Afrekete] was bigger than she actually was, because there was a comfortable smell about her that I always associated with large women" (243). By mythologizing Afrekete as fat, Lorde renders her an even more potent spiritual symbol, suggesting her resourcefulness and productive capacity liken her to ancient fertility fetishes.[47]

Afrekete's introduction into the narrative as well as her spiritual significance is foreshadowed in a scene where Lorde boards a bus at a crossroads. Cassie Premo Steele suggests that "[t]his scene prefigures Lorde's transformation of her own African, Caribbean, African American, Christian background into the new self" and that "Afrekete functions as the conduit for the healing of all the different aspects of Lorde's history" (85).[48] This healing, both sexual and cultural, begins at the party where Lorde and Afrekete initiate their relationship. They dance to a variety of songs, including a Belafonte calypso and a Sinatra waltz, mirroring the cultural milieu from which Lorde has evolved (245).[49] As the relationship develops, Afrekete takes Lorde on a gastronomic expedition, visiting the West Indian markets and Puerto Rican bodegas from which Afrekete buys a range of tropical produce, including plantains and avocado that end up being incorporated into their lovemaking (249, 251). The use of these food items for sexual pleasure prefigures the amalgamation of Lorde's sexual and cultural self, which Afrekete facilitates.

In a scene near the end of the text, Lorde narrates a sexual encounter that takes place on the roof of Afrekete's apartment building. The couple's naked bodies are bathed in silvery moonlight, implying that as lesbian women they have a healthy and natural connection with nature and rebutting hegemonic imperatives of heterosexuality. Additionally, the coating of their bodies in moon rays infers a sort of matriarchal baptism, further suggesting that the sexual experience has a simultaneous spiritual component. In describing the encounter, Lorde slips into a second person narrative, which resembles a prayerful petition, and addresses Afrekete, further establishing Afrekete's divinity: "Afrekete, Afrekete ride me to the crossroads where we shall sleep, coated in the woman's power. The sound of our bodies meeting is the prayer of all strangers and sisters, that the discarded evils, abandoned at all crossroads, will not follow us upon our journeys" (252).

While Lorde's configuration of Afrekete as a divine entity defies Judeo-Christian monotheism, perhaps Lorde's ultimate act of insubordination towards Western patriarchal ideals rests with the act of narrating her history. By claiming her African, Afro-Caribbean, and African American cultural identity as well as her lesbian sexual identity and grounding these as the framework of the biomythographical account of her life, Lorde insists upon the validity and viability of these components of herself in the face of a sociopolitical environment that negated those identities as she grew up. Furthermore, Lorde's acknowledgment and acceptance of her fatness is yet another aspect of her rebellious narrative. She affronts traditional notions of beauty and sexual appeal by sharing the sexual adventures of a fat, black woman, indeed by even allowing her character to exist as a sexual agent. By incorporating her large body into her self-portrayal, Lorde furthers her task of decentering Western imperialist ideologies and renegotiating sexual and narrative space for the various marginalized components of herself.

The history of Jamaican national hero Nanny of the Maroons is also a narrative about the renegotiation of space—literal and figurative space. This legendary figure, who came to fame in the first half of the eighteenth century, straddles the gap between the real and the mystical. Nanny is famed for her successful negotiations with the British for five hundred acres of land awarded to her and her people in 1741 in the parish of Portland.[50] She was a runaway slave who escaped, fleeing into the remote Jamaican mountainside where she eventually assumed military and spiritual leadership of other refugees known as Maroons.[51] She was a superb military strategist who managed to persistently outwit the British soldiers until they eventually offered her a peace treaty that she hesitantly accepted.[52] However, Nanny's infamy extends beyond her military prowess.

Nanny was also a famed obeah woman, purportedly able to magically conceal her village with a spell that has lingered into present times.[53] Some of her other supernatural attributes include maintaining a huge pot that bubbled without any fire and drew British soldiers to their death in the fiery cauldron.[54] Maroon oral history records that Nanny was given divine instructions "to plant pumpkin seeds in her pocket. Miraculously, the seeds sprouted and bore fruit almost overnight, enabling the hard-pressed Maroons to sustain themselves and regroup under Nanny's leadership" (Olsen 234). But Nanny's most interesting magical talent was her "ability to catch the bullets of the soldiers with her posterior and hurl them back at her assailants in an obscene but effective manner" (Tuelon 21).

While historical records do not describe Nanny as a fat woman, the use of her fleshy buttocks in an act of rebellion firmly places her as a viable entity in the discussion of the fat black woman's sexuality. The historical legacy of the black woman's derrière as a potent sexual icon further inscribes Nanny's bodily talent as an important part of this project and her bodily unruliness makes her an appropriate figure with which to conclude this chapter.

Nanny's mythical skill prefigures the resistance of Nichols' fat black woman to the Western beauty aesthetic as Nanny defies not only British law but natural law by returning her enemy's bullets. Like Winkler's Miss B, Nanny is also associated with abundance, and the sexual trope of planting seeds in her pockets to feed her followers offers the subtle suggestion that sexuality provides human nurturance beyond the realm of satisfying reproductive needs. Angelou's phenomenal woman also grounds her quasi-supernatural talents that she names as her "inner mystery" in her large, fleshy body (Angelou 131). Similar to Nanny, the phenomenal woman's potency rests in the metaphorical resistance of her fat anatomy, and just as Nanny's butt functions as a buffer against imperialist aggression, the "span" of the phenomenal woman's hips frame sexual organs—the place where her "secret" is ensconced (Angelou 130).

The historical narratives surrounding Nanny's life are rife with absences and vague particulars; some events such as the grant of the land patent are documented while other information such as her marital status and magical talents are not. Lorde's narrative indirectly responds to these gaps in Nanny's life and the lives of many black women by providing a detailed narration of Lorde's history, grounding it in her body's sexual adventures and evolution. Lorde's response appropriates her fat black body as a source of epistemological value since this body is the means through which she understands and encounters the neocolonial forces that would seek to render her as inauthentic. Nanny's abstract, fat buttocks enter the conversation on issues of race and gender by exposing an alternate magical realm of bodily knowledge and resistance. And Nanny's sexually obscene response enacted with her fleshy derrière is mirrored in Lorde's narrative of what the white hegemony would conceive of as sexual deviance and unruliness enacted using her fat black body.

This chapter's study of literary and cultural representations of the full-bodied black woman suggests that her size and race fuse together to hypersexualize her image. Her hypersexuality becomes a deployable trope for disobedience and disruptiveness, most often targeted at Western cultural ideology that marginalizes on the basis of race and gender. However, the unruliness that underscores this resistance is somewhat problematic because while its antagonism towards marginalizing agendas is apparent, this antagonism may also be read as a reconfirmation of *The Malleus Maleficarum*'s suggestion that women are "defective" beings and unnatural freaks. Moreover, like the Venus Hottentot, the fat black woman's sexual resistance might be contextualized by a Eurocentric assumption that blackness is equivalent to sexual lasciviousness, which situates her sexuality as a sort of primitivism.

However, the modern textual and popular representations of the fat black woman throughout the African Diaspora are polyvalent in their antagonism towards racist and sexist ideologies and they achieve this capacity by intertwining multiple planes of resistance on the site of the large black female body. As the chapter previously suggests, the large female body is at times masculinized, and this reversal of gender norms adds a certain measure of resonance to that body's resistance because it recognizes the gendered disparity regarding the way sexual privilege is dispensed in Western culture. This masculinizing metaphor underscores another portion of this chapter's argument: that the fat black woman is often represented in African diasporic literature as engaging in sexual pleasure for its own sake and not because of any reproductive imperatives. This perspective on sexuality is especially apparent in Lorde's biomythography, which celebrates lesbian sexuality, and also in *The Duppy*, where Miss B glorifies sexuality as a divine ritual. Additionally, all of the texts in which this chapter is anchored incorporate verbal rebellion as a core characteristic of the fat black female characters.

Finally, the fat black woman's sexuality is sometimes positioned in tandem with her culture's other sexual issues and beyond the scope of her individual behavior. As a result her "freakishness" is resituated from the site of her body onto the site of the popular body politic and becomes a reflection of her culture's sexual taboos. Her body is a venue for the expression of cultural anxieties related to bodily transgression, particularly those that are sexual, because the Judeo-Christian ethos, which underlies Western culture, has only created safe spaces to engage normative sexuality—heterosexual sex in a monogamously framed relationship underscored by the goal of creating a family. The fat black woman's body has become a convenient cultural target for this displaced sexual anxiety because in its triply marginalized state, it diverts attention from deviant, male-centered sexuality. Furthermore, the lack of social and political power among similar bodies in the culture limits the ability for large black women to confront and contest these hypersexualized representations.

Despite the absence of actualized political power, the fat black woman is able to harness strength from the erotic by reveling in her fatness and blackness all at the same time—aware of her sexuality and not ashamed of it. Lorde understands the erotic as "an assertion of the life force of women," and textual representations of fat black women amalgamate sexual desire/appeal and the aspiration for cultural and political viability.[55] This combination is achieved through parallel constructions of the world as with *The Duppy* or parallel constructions of identity as with *The Fat*

Black Woman's Poems. This harnessing of the erotic is achieved through the disavowal of Western beauty imperatives—this rejection is a necessary postcolonial survival strategy—and the narratives the chapter surveys suggest that consequentially the fat black woman in her triply displaced constituency is ideally poised to survive the ravages of her postcolonial legacy. The literary characters discussed in this chapter reflect this endurance and resistive capacity, which they are given through the metaphorical link between fatness and sexuality as potent forces in the disruption of neocolonial endeavors of marginalization.

NOTES

1. *The Life and Times of Sara Baartman the Hottentot Venus*, directed by Zola Maseko, First Run/Icarus Films, 1998.
2. *The Life and Times of Sara Baartman the Hottentot Venus*. Baartman died at the age of twenty-five.
3. *The Life and Times of Sara Baartman the Hottentot Venus*.
4. Myriam Chancy, "The Black Female Body as Popular Icon," *Essays on Transgressive Readings: Reading Over Lines*, ed. Georgia Johnston (Lewiston, N.Y.: Mellen, 1997), 95–117.
5. Erin J. Aubry, "The Butt: Its Politics, Its Profanity, Its Power," *Body Outlaws*, ed. Ophira Edut (New York: Seal Press, 2000), 22–31.
6. Sander L. Gilman, "Black Bodies, White Bodies: Toward an Iconography of Female Sexuality in Late Nineteenth-Century Art, Medicine, and Literature," *"Race," Writing, and Difference*, ed. Henry Louis Gates Jr. (Chicago: The University of Chicago Press, 1986), 232.
7. Gilman, "Black Bodies, White Bodies," 231–32. Gilman discusses a number of scientists, including J. J Virey, Georges Cuvier, and Henri de Blainville, whose research positions black women as anatomically abnormal and their sexuality as "primitive."
8. Zine Magubane, "Which Bodies Matter? Feminism, Poststructuralism, Race, and the Curious Theoretical Odyssey of the 'Hottentot Venus,'" *Gender & Society: Official Publication of Sociologists of Women in Society* 15, no. 6 (2001): 816–34. In this thoughtfully crafted essay, Magubane challenges Gilman's suggestion that Baartman was the embodiment of blackness and difference, questioning if such an embodiment is even possible, and instead proposes that it is our acceptance of Gilman's argument that has made Baartman come to represent all these things Gilman suggests. Furthermore, Magubane contends that Gilman's ideas assume that the construction of blackness was/is stable, citing Celts as being considered black by nineteenth-century standards. Magubane further argues that Gilman implies that all of Europe felt the same regarding black sexuality. While Magubane's argument is sound, I believe that Baartman's current iconographic status among scholars as a marker of otherness still merits our consideration of her. Whether or not Gilman is historically accurate and Baartman signified in this way during her lifetime is not for me as consequential as the ease with which so many scholars

have unquestioningly embraced Gilman's ideas and accepted Baartman as the marker of otherness in our time, indicating our belief that this is what she represents.

9. Linus Abraham, "The Black Woman as Marker of Hypersexuality in Western Mythology: A Contemporary Manifestation in the Film *The Scarlet Letter*," *Journal of Communication Inquiry* 26, no. 2 (April 2002): 201.

10. bell hooks, "Selling Hot Pussy: Representations of Black Female Sexuality in the Cultural Marketplace," *Writing on the Body*, eds. Katie Conboy, Nadia Medina and Sarah Stanbury (New York: Columbia University Press, 1997), 115.

11. hooks, "Selling Hot Pussy," 115.

12. hooks, "Selling Hot Pussy," 122.

13. hooks, "Selling Hot Pussy," 119.

14. Mary Condé, "Fat Women and Food," *Beyond the Pleasure Dome: Writing From the Romantics*, ed. Sue Vice, Matthew Campbell, and Tim Armstrong (Sheffield: Sheffield Academic Press, 1994), 124–31. Condé notes that "fatness is often linked to the examination of race in fiction" (126).

15. Sigmund Freud, *The Basic Writings of Sigmund Freud*, ed. and trans. A. A. Brill ((New York: Random House, 1938), 566.

16. Jana Evans Braziel, "Sex and Fat Chics: Deterritorializing the Fat Female Body," *Bodies Out of Bounds: Fatness and Transgression*, eds. Jana Evans Braziel and Kathleen LeBesco (Berkeley: University of California Press, 2001), 233.

17. Gilman, "Black Bodies, White Bodies," 243.

18. Tania Modleski, "Cinema and the Dark Continent: Race and Gender in Popular Film," *Writing on the Body*, eds. Katie Conboy, Nadia Medina, and Sarah Stanbury (New York: Columbia University Press, 1997), 221.

19. Modleski, "Cinema and the Dark Continent," 221.

20. Modleski, "Cinema and the Dark Continent," 221.

21. Susan Bordo, *Unbearable Weight: Feminism, Western Culture, and the Body* (Berkeley: University of California Press, 1993), 230. See Bordo's discussion of Victorian handbooks as an archetype for modern cultural requirements regarding female consumption of food.

22. "'The Parkers' Win Big Laughs as No. 1 Show in Black Households," *Jet* (April 10, 2000): 58, Expanded Academic ASAP, Infotrac, University of Miami, accessed November 3, 2003, <http://web3.infotrac.galegroup.com>.

23. Susan Schindehette, "Kermit, Miss Piggy, Big Bird, Grover and Kids All Over the World Mourn the Loss of Muppetmeister Jim Henson," *People Weekly* (May 28, 1990): 119, Expanded Academic ASAP, Infotrac, University of Miami, accessed November 3, 2003, <http://web3.infotrac.galegroup.com>.

24. "Oh Sow Chic," *Time* (November 2, 1998): 115, Expanded Academic ASAP, Infotrac, University of Miami, accessed November 3, 2003, <http://web3.infotrac.galegroup.com>; "Miss Piggy Stars in Baked Lay's Ad," *The New York Times*, August 2, 1996: 22, Expanded Academic ASAP, Infotrac, University of Miami, accessed November 3, 2003, <http://web3.infotrac.galegroup.com>; "Miss Piggy Goes Hog Wild for Denny's Restaurants," *Brandweek* (May 20, 2002): 5, Expanded Academic ASAP, Infotrac, University of Miami, accessed November 3, 2003, <http://web3.infotrac.galegroup.com>.

25. Angela Stukator, "'It's Not Over Until The Fat Lady Sings' : Comedy, and the Carnivalesque, and Body Politics," *Bodies Out of Bounds: Fatness and Transgres-*

sion, eds. Jana Evans Braziel and Kathleen LeBesco (Berkeley: University of California Press, 2001), 197–213.

26. Aristotle, *Generation of Animals*, trans. A. L. Peck (Cambridge, Mass.: Harvard University Press, 1953).

27. Rosi Braaidotti, "Mothers, Monsters and Machines," *Writing on the Body*, eds. Katie Conboy, Nadia Medina, and Sarah Stanbury (New York: Columbia University Press, 1997), 64.

28. Moira Gatens, "Corporeal Representations in/and the Body Politic," *Writing on the Body*, eds. Katie Conboy, Nadia Medina, and Sarah Stanbury (New York: Columbia University Press, 1997), 84.

29. Heinrich Kramer and James Sprenger, *The Malleus Maleficarum*, trans. Montague Summers (New York: Dover Publications, 1971).

30. Montague Summers, "Introduction to the 1948 Edition," *The Malleus Maleficarum*, by Heinrich Kramer and James Sprenger, trans. Montague Summers (New York: Dover Publications, 1971), v–x.

31. Gatens, "Corporeal Representations in/and the Body Politic," 84.

32. Hazel V. Carby, *Cultures in Babylon* (London: Verso, 1999), 24.

33. Le'a Kent, "Fighting Abjection: Representing Fat Women," *Bodies Out of Bounds: Fatness and Transgression*, eds. Jana Evans Braziel and Kathleen LeBesco (Berkeley: University of California Press, 2001), 130–52.

34. Maya Angelou, "Phenomenal Woman," *The Complete Collected Poems of Maya Angelou* (New York: Random House, 1994), 130.

35. Brent Cunningham, "Maya Angelou: Best-selling Poet Shares Story of Her Life and Work, " *University of Buffalo Reporter*, April 30, 1998, accessed April 17, 2003, <www.buffalo.edu/reporter/vol29/vol29n30/n3.html>.

36. The term also invokes the Hottentot Venus and her condition of steatopygia.

37. Alison Easton, "The Body as History and 'Writing the Body': The Example of Grace Nichols," *Journal of Gender Studies* 3, no. 1 (March 1994), *Academic Search Elite*, EBSCO, University of Miami, accessed September 12, 2003, <www.weblinks2.epnet.com>.

38. Kim Chernin, *The Obsession: Reflections on the Tyranny of Slenderness* (New York: Harper & Row, 1981).

39. Grace Nichols, "The Battle with Language," *Caribbean Women Writers: Essays From the First International Conference*, ed. Selwyn R. Cudjoe (Wellesley, Mass.: Calaloux Publications, 1990), 283–89.

40. Sandra Lee Bartky, "Foucault, Femininity, and the Modernization of Patriarchal Power," *Writing on the Body*, eds. Katie Conboy, Nadia Medina, and Sarah Stanbury (New York: Columbia University Press, 1997), 129–54.

41. "Duppy" is a Jamaican term for ghost.

42. Miss B's celebration of sexuality also resonates in Jamaican dancehall music, known for its foregrounding and glorification of sex.

43. See chapter three for a more detailed discussion of the fat female body as a metaphor for economic wealth.

44. Kim Robinson-Walcott, "Carnival Meets Dancehall: Winkler's Vision of Heaven in *The Duppy*," *Sargasso* 10 (2000): 25–37.

45. "Julius and Ethel Rosenberg (Summary)," *Freedom of Information Act*, FBI, accessed November 28, 2003, <http://foia.fbi.gov/roberg.htm>.

46. This process of renaming pagan gods also occurs in religious practices such as Voodoo and Santeria, in which Yoruban Orishas are given the names of Catholic saints.

47. See the introduction for a discussion of the Venus of Willendorf.

48. Cassie Steele, "Remembering 'The Great Mother of Us All': Audre Lorde's Journey Through History to Herself," *Gendered Memories* (Rodopi: Amsterdam, 2000), 77–88.

49. Steele, "Remembering 'The Great Mother of Us All,'" 85.

50. Lucille Mathurin Mair, "Recollections of a Journey into a Rebel Past," *Caribbean Women Writers: Essays From the First International Conference*, ed. Selwyn R. Cudjoe (Wellesley, Mass.: Calaloux Publications, 1990), 51–60. Mair explains that the Maroons still reside on the property secured for them by Nanny.

51. Mair, "Recollections of a Journey into a Rebel Past," 57. In another account of Nanny's life, Eric P. Olsen explains that Maroon oral history suggests that Nanny came from royalty and was never a slave but that she and her family were "banished" to Jamaica. See Eric P. Olsen, "Mountain Rebels: Nanny of the Maroons," *World and I* 15, no. 2 (Feb. 2000): 234.

52. Olsen, "Mountain Rebels," 234.

53. Alan Tuelon, "Nanny—Maroon Chieftainess," *Caribbean Quarterly* 19, no. 4 (1973): 20–27. Tuelon explains that several groups that have tried to locate the ruins of Nanny Town have had unusual experiences during their expedition to find the town, some becoming lost and never reaching their destination (24).

54. Tuelon, "Nanny—Maroon Chieftainess," 21.

55. Audre Lorde, "Uses of the Erotic: The Erotic as Power," *Sister Outsider: Essay and Speeches by Audre Lorde* (Freedom, Calif.: Crossing Press, 1984), 53–59.

3

Bodily Abundance

Female obsession with weight seems to be following an inversely proportional trajectory relative to the strides women have made towards social and economic independence.[1] Furthermore, despite the billions we spend each year in an effort to lose weight, few of us ever achieve our ideal bodily goal.[2] In her book *The Beauty Myth,* Naomi Wolf evaluates the oppressive function of beauty in our society, and she suggests that women's ever-increasing obsession with body size is a consequence of the recent academic and professional growth they have experienced:

> More women have more money and power and scope and legal recognition than we have ever had before; but in terms of how we feel about ourselves *physically*, we may actually be worse off than our unliberated grandmothers. It is no accident that so many potentially powerful women feel this way. We are in the midst of a violent backlash against feminism that uses images of female beauty as a political weapon against women's advancement: the beauty myth. (10)

The outcome of the beauty myth is that many women are unable to feel complete satisfaction with their lives, even after achieving the most outstanding personal and professional success. Talk-show host Oprah Winfrey, one of the wealthiest and most famous women in America, has named her weight loss of sixty-seven pounds as the most "significant achievement of her life" (Oprah qtd. in Bordo 60).[3]

Oprah's comment is an intriguing one, and it consolidates my interest in the way fatness and economic circumstances are conjoined throughout the African Diaspora. How is it that Oprah's weight loss outstrips the magnitude of her economic accomplishments? This chapter explores fatness within an economic context and considers the ways in which the fat black woman's body is juxtaposed with images of material wealth in both literary and popular representations. The robust black woman's body is often presented as an icon for material abundance in contrast to the African Diaspora's historical legacy of economic oppression, deprivation and material loss in multiple arenas. Furthermore, within the context of a postcolonial culture's poverty stricken economic landscape, fatness becomes a form of neocolonial currency that signifies wealth despite the presence of national and racial indicators of economic decline and atrophy. The fat black woman's body continues to maintain its social and iconic acceptability throughout the African Diaspora in the face of prevailing imperatives of slenderness in part because of the legacy of slavery in which that body is anchored. This legacy is epitomized by loss, including the loss of homeland, the loss of self-autonomy, and the loss of loved ones through the sale and dispersal of slave families and later through immigration.

In a project like this one that concentrates on body size, one of the most meaningful historical demarcations of loss is the deprivation of food to which slaves were subjected. In the Caribbean, a significant portion of the slaves' food supply was imported from the American colonies, and when this supply was interrupted because of natural disasters such as hurricanes, slaves would sometimes starve to death.[4] Furthermore, Caribbean slave rations, which usually consisted of preserved fish or meat along with some type of grain, did not supply adequate calories or nutrients, and slaves were often deficient in calcium, vitamin A, and thiamine.[5] In America, slave rations mostly consisted of cornmeal, rice, pork fat, and salted pork meat.[6] The poor nutritional content of this diet made slaves susceptible to diseases such as rickets, beriberi, and scurvy.[7]

Perhaps this history in addition to income-based restricted access to diet aids accounts for the disproportionately lower incidence of eating disorders among black women in contrast to their higher than proportionate levels of obesity.[8] Furthermore, black women have fewer anxieties pertaining to body image, and their marginalization within the dominant culture's beauty arena is partially responsible. In response to this marginalization, black women have been forced to develop an alternate self-relational context in which the Euro-feminine ideal is diluted and modified. The existence of this substitute beauty reality is evident in a study of body image among American girls. The survey revealed that while 90 percent of white girls were dissatisfied with their size, 70 percent of black girls were comfortable with themselves as they were.[9] The increased unwillingness of black women to starve their bodies and their resistance to imperatives of slenderness are connected to both their history of food deprivation and to the widespread cultural acceptance throughout the African Diaspora for the fleshy black female body. However, the emblematic value of this fat body extends beyond the aesthetic realm.

Karl Marx's economic theory of surplus value provides a two-dimensional metaphorical paradigm that illuminates the cultural connotations of female fatness in the black Diaspora. On a literal plane Marx's theory specifically addresses the "theft" of labor from workers, and nowhere in recent history is this act of economic aggression more apparent than with regard to slavery. In *Capital: A Critique of Political Economy*, Marx explains that capital (C) consists of two elements: "constant capital" (c), which is the money expended on the "means of production," and "variable capital" (v), the money spent for labor (235).[10] For example, in the case of a slave sugar plantation, c might consist of the cost of farming equipment, agricultural supplies and so on, while v would not include any wages—just the cost of purchasing, and maintaining the slaves. In fact, just as slave owners often indicated by their accounting practices, the slaves could arguably be considered farming machinery, eliminating v entirely. Once a commodity is produced, its value can then be conceived of as $(c + v) + s$, s being the surplus value of that commodity, or in other words, the profit made by the owner of the capital.[11] According to Marx, "The rate of surplus value is therefore an exact expression for the degree of exploitation of labour-power by capital, or of the labourer by the capitalist" (241). Marx's ideas add another facet to the perception of slavery and its ongoing legacy of racist, neocolonial, economic aggression by quantifying oppression.

This notion of surplus value is crucial to this project because it provides the framework for reading the fat black woman's body. In response to her diasporic legacy of loss and deprivation, the large black woman's fat is an establishment of her privately owned surplus value. In a very literal sense, fat provides a bulwark against the ultimate physiological deprivation: the shortage of food. Furthermore, fatness is also a metaphor for access to resources as well as a rebuttal of Western hegemonic efforts to decorporealize the black body through that body's marginalization and the rendering of that body as invisible. By boasting a physiology that rejects some dominant presumptions of blackness—invisibility and the inability to manage and accumulate resources—the large black woman's body becomes a compelling form of anti-colonial currency. Furthermore, the black woman's body is a particularly appropriate site for resistance since it must challenge two forms of marginalization based upon both race and gender.

In some African cultures the large woman's bodily connotation of material abundance and surplus value has tremendous symbolic resonance. This aesthetic appreciation of the large female body is probably one of the primary contributors to the African Diaspora's cultural acceptance of large women. In fact, the value attached to the copious woman's body is so pronounced that depictions of female slimness in African literature often function as a trope for desexualization.[12] Furthermore, the tradition of sending young women to "fatting houses" in preparation for marriage consolidates the African aesthetic appreciation of the fat female body. The term "fatting house," although self-explanatory, is probably inconceivable in our era of twenty-four hour fitness centers and liposuction; however, these houses were designed for the literal purpose of "fattening" girls to make them more aesthetically pleasing and more viable brides. While fatting houses may seem like a remote ritual from Africa's distant history, it is a rite of passage that continues to be practiced today.

The film *Monday's Girls*, released in 1994, documents a group of young women's experiences as they sojourn five weeks in an African fatting house.[13] Set in the small fishing village of Ogoloma, Nigeria—population twenty thousand—the group of initiates is handed over to the care of an older woman named Monday Moses. As they prepare to enter the fatting house, one girl expresses her desire to become as fat as possible, while another initiate's family plans to take her extra food to accelerate her weight gain. Additionally, the initiates' legs are bound in coiled metal to restrict movement and further encourage their bodies to become fat. During the course of their time with Monday, the girls are not only fed well, they are taught about men and motherhood and encouraged to be submissive and grateful to their spouses. After several weeks, when Monday decides the girls' confinement is complete, they leave the fatting house in a lavish ceremony attended by some twelve thousand spectators—over half of their village.

The fatting house ritual is a powerful indication that alternative aesthetic paradigms exist, and as such they may be read as "anti-colonial" currency because they do not privilege Western values. However, the fatting house is simultaneously a problematic metaphor because its existence signals yet another bid to control female behavior under the auspices of beauty, not unlike the current Western beauty dictates and their subsequent complications that arise from imperatives of slenderness. In her novel *The Fattening Hut*, Pat Lowery Collins fashions the fatting house as a torturous ritual that sets the symbolic precedence for married life—one of conformity to patriarchal restrictions over women's behavior.[14] In Collins' text, her protagonist is so disturbed by her confinement in a fatting house that she loses her appetite and must be "rescued" as a means of avoiding the limitations that marriage denotes.

As we enter the new millennium, the fatting house ritual seems to be transforming into a more symbolic than functional ceremony since not all of the girls under Monday's care are prepared to marry immediately, and several state educational aspirations that they plan to fulfill before becoming a wife. However, while the ritual illustrates that the culture actively maintains space to delineate female behavior, the ceremony also marks its continued embrace of corpulence, clearly demarcating a West African aesthetic divergence from Western cultural norms. This aesthetic divergence is not unique to Western Africa, and the orchestrated fattening of women to enhance their aesthetic appeal and fertility have been observed in Polynesia, as well as in Mauritania and Tunisia.[15] The fatting house emerges as an important icon for this project as it represents the programmed dedication of resources for the physiological benefit of women, further anchoring the fat black woman's body as a metaphor for surplus value. Moreover, the fatting house ritual of strictly limiting the labor output of initiates, which in effect temporarily makes the participants operate with the leisure of plantation mistresses, reaffirms the representational status of the fat black woman's body as a site of resistance to economic aggression.[16]

In the Caribbean, the robust female body is also regarded as a naturalization of access to resources, and certain large black women have become historical icons associated with financial opportunity and an abundance of nurturance, specifically Jamaican nurse, entrepreneur and writer Mary Seacole, and Barbadian lodging-house keeper Rachel Pringle.[17] Pringle has not only been portrayed as a fleshy woman, but her corpulence is particularly well anchored as a component of her persona in depictions of her ample body on a variety of souvenirs, which abound in Barbadian gift shops. Posters of her are even available online.

Pringle, who is legendary in Barbadian history for her outstanding accumulation of wealth, operated lodging-houses, and quite likely ran at least one of her properties—The Royal Naval Hotel—as a brothel.[18] She was the offspring of an African mother and Scottish father, who operated a shop in Bridgetown and exposed Rachel from an early age to the inner workings of the entrepreneurial sphere.[19] However, reports are that her father attempted to sexually molest Rachel, who was eventually rescued from him by Thomas Pringle—a British naval officer.[20] Pringle helped establish Rachel in the hospitality industry, and at the height of her career, she even entertained Prince William Henry (who later became King William IV) at one of her establishments.[21] Initial references to Rachel in the Barbadian Levy Books (tax records) indicate that in 1779 she owned only one property; however, by 1783 she owned two, and by 1788 she was being assessed for taxes on a total of five holdings.[22] At the time of her death in 1791, Rachel "owned at least nineteen slaves, a substantial number for a person of any racial group living in an urban area" (Sweet and Nash 187).

Images of Seacole indicate that she was also a fleshy woman, and like Pringle, Seacole also ran lodging-houses at various points in her life.[23] In her autobiography, *The Wonderful Adventures of Mrs. Seacole in Many Lands*, she recounts the diverse healing expeditions and entrepreneurial endeavors that characterized her unique life.[24] From her adventures in Panama where she helped fight epidemics of cholera and yellow fever to her involvement in the Crimean War, during which she cared for British soldiers at her "hotel," Seacole's persona was consistently associated with the provision of health care and the pursuit of entrepreneurial opportunities. While operating the British Hotel in the Crimea, she cared for men afflicted with a range of illnesses, including dysentery, diarrhea and jaundice, and several of her patients wrote testimonials of her service to them. In her autobiography, Seacole records the accounts of a former patient:

> I have much pleasure in bearing testimony to Mrs. Seacole's kindness and attention to the sick of the Railway Labourers' Army Works Corps and Land Transport Corps during the winters of 1854 and 1855.
>
> She not only, from the knowledge she acquired in the West Indies, was enabled to administer appropriate remedies for their ailments, but what was of as much or more importance, she charitably furnished them with proper nourishment. . . . (Seacole 129–30)

Furthermore, her life was one of relative prosperity for a black, Caribbean woman, despite some periods of financial instability.[25] Seacole's access to capital was evident from her numerous expeditions, and when the British government repeatedly denied her request to join Florence Nightingale and other nurses in the Crimea, Seacole funded the long journey with her own money.[26]

Similar to her forebears, Seacole and Pringle, the Caribbean higgler has earned the reputation as an adept and determined full-figured entrepreneur, and as with Seacole, mobility has become the hallmark of this successful group of traders. "Higglering" has its roots in the Caribbean slave economy and was also known as huckstering.[27] Originally higglers were predominantly slave women who engaged in the informal trade of produce, traveling between the rural areas and the urban city centers, and despite their restrictive social status as slaves, they were frequently an ardent source of competition for other merchants.[28] In Jamaica, the provision grounds cultivated by slave women became such an important component of the country's internal economy that even the white diet was sustained by the food these women supplied.[29] In Barbados where the slaves were not allotted land for independent agro-economic pursuits, they grew food on the property surrounding their dwellings.[30] On Sundays, when they often had time off, slave women traveled around Barbados to attend Sunday market, many bearing baskets on their heads.[31]

This image of the Caribbean market woman is a pervasive one, heavily invested with cultural significance as an icon of Caribbean womanhood and extensively commodified for local and international consumption. Representations of market women suffuse theatrical productions and adorn every imaginable Caribbean souvenir, including postcards, tourism promotions, and even tea towels. Moreover, the national costume of Jamaica, worn at international beauty contests by the nation's representatives, seems to derive from the clothing in which market women are often portrayed. The pageant outfit features a long, colorful madras-print skirt that is typically ruffled and quite full, creating the same bulky look of the skirts and aprons that vendors usually wear. The rest of the costume includes a peasant blouse that is commonly white and the ubiquitous accessory appropriated for all renderings of market women: a head tie.

The higgler's image and the nature of her trade have evolved over the course of the Caribbean's history, and one variety of the higgler's most recent incarnations is the international merchant. Known in Jamaica as ICIs (informal commercial importers) and in Barbados as "suitcase traders," these vendors continue to be predominantly women, and they travel to places as varied as Panama, Puerto Rico, the Cayman Islands and Miami to procure merchandise for resale in their homeland.[32] Interestingly, the image of a higgler that has evolved in the Caribbean imagination typically features a fat and rambunctious woman, her historical association with food mirrored by her fleshiness.[33] Furthermore, the higgler's ample body underscores her iconographic status as Afro-Caribbean womanhood since her fatness is an evocation of her blackness.

In several articles written during the 1980s for the Jamaican newspaper *The Gleaner*, columnist Morris Cargill offered a controversial portrayal of the Jamaican higgler, a frequent target of his social commentary. He asserts the anomalous nature of the higgler, specifically locating her large body as the source of deviance: "Considering that so many Jamaican girls are slim and pretty," Cargill begins one of his columns, "one is bound to wonder whether higglers are the result of some sort of selective breeding" (28).[34] Cargill establishes slenderness as normative, instantly marginalizing the higgler based on his construction of her body as a divergence from his Euro-feminine ideal. Additionally, his use of the term "breeding" evokes slavery's reproductive oppression, situating the higgler as a specular shadow of the slave woman. He mystifies the higgler's body as a strategy to avoid engaging the sociopolitical context that has fostered the need for her extensive labor output:

> [F]ew [higglers] seem to weigh less than 250 lbs. They are also a special shape, sticking out back and front simultaneously: huge protruding bottoms and equally huge tops, both of which they use as battering rams.

> Run up against a higgler, or worse still have one run up against you and you soon know that there is no soft, flabby fat there, but solid muscle, and no dancer is quicker on her feet.
>
> How do they get that shape and size, and from quite an early age too? (29)

Cargill's persistence in the colonial tradition of de-feminizing the black woman's body diverts our attention from the enormity of her entrepreneurial endeavors, asking us to focus instead on the purported enormity of her body.[35] Even the language he employs to discuss the higglers' trading activities further exposes his disdain for these women. He describes them and their luggage as a "menace" and explains that they do damage to the shopping plazas they "infest" in order to sell their merchandise (28–29).

But is Cargill's disregard for these women and his contempt for their size based simply upon the perceived inconvenience their trading activities pose to him, or is it sustained by a more entrenched scorn that rests with the socioeconomic status and race their supposedly large black bodies signify? Gina Ulysse dichotomizes representations of Jamaican femininity with the terms "uptown lady" and "downtown women," using the spatial differentiation of the suburbs versus the inner city to demarcate socioeconomic boundaries and to attach specific engagements of femininity to each region.[36] Ulysse asserts that indelicate behavior and dark skin (and I would add a fat body) are qualities that are associated with the geographic region of "downtown." The female identity associated with this vulgar arena is "woman" as opposed to "lady," which is reserved for women who qualify for that title via a blend of behavioral and physiological qualities. Ulysse also suggests that the upper classes perceive a higgler as "a large, dark-skinned uneducated woman who wears loud clothes, heavy jewelry and occupies too much space" (276).

Cargill, who looks white, refers to himself as "slightly Off White," suggesting his mixed ancestry (27). However, when he expresses his disenchantment with higglers, he reflects a "pure" replication of the Caribbean bourgeoisie's neocolonial angst, provoked by the higgler's efforts toward the reclamation of that surplus value stolen from her foremothers. The essence of Cargill's diatribes against the higgler is that she literally "occupies too much space." Her large body, her luggage, and her goods sprawled on Kingston's sidewalks are all an extension of her massive girth and like her body, a material representation of abundance as well as her access to capital. Through her importing activities she inhabits economic space, and when she travels, she takes up social space reserved for the Caribbean's elite, and this is the source of the higgler's actual transgressions against Cargill, not her fat body. Furthermore, colonialist ventures have always featured infringement on other people's space, so the higgler effectively reverses the process with her large and intrusive body.

A trope of equivalency, similar to what Cargill sets up, occurs in African American women's literature, and in this genre the black woman's large body corresponds to both material wealth and paranormal abundance. The coupling of these characteristics may seem incongruous; however, accumulating wealth and accumulating magical skills must bare a striking resemblance to people living under extremely oppressive economic circumstances. Even those of us with college degrees and middle-class incomes have difficulty grasping the net worth of billionaires Oprah Winfrey and Bill Gates, and it is somewhere in this seemingly infinite gap between us and them that the notions of wealth and magic become synonymous.

In Gloria Naylor's *Mama Day*, magic is the novel's primary currency. Set on the mythical Sea Island of Willow Springs, where the entire population is African American, the novel fashions traditional folk-magic as a form of neocolonial resistance to the encroaching cultural values of the dominant white majority on the mainland of nearby Georgia and South Carolina. The eccentric blend of residents who comprise this small island community have a deeply rooted recognition of the spirit world. Mama Day, a woman of renowned magical prowess, is the novel's central character and the de facto matriarch of Willow Springs, but she is not the only resident of the community who is proficient in magic. Ruby, a very large woman, is also steeped in the supernatural, and her ample body is a trope for her magical talent.

Described as having "arms and legs almost thick around as small tree trunks" and "a middle that is as wide as the old oak down by Chevy's Pass," Ruby's tremendous body is as legendary as her skill at working "roots" (134). The crafting of Ruby's physical description using allusions to a tree suggests she is a sort of mystical hybrid who integrates both human and non-human characteristics. The communal narrator of the text further explains that Ruby's ample body even transcends traditional notions of fatness: "you couldn't rightly call Ruby fat—she's amazing. Nothing jiggles when she walks or gushes out of her clothes. Whatever she puts into her mouth turns into solid meat and is distributed even-like on all six feet of her" (134). Ruby's height and command over her massive girth both underscore her supernatural abilities, implying that she has a similar control over them.

However, rumor in Willow Springs has it that Ruby misuses her magical knowledge, displaces herself as a benevolent Big Mamma, and instead enacts the role of a malicious agent of avarice. The color that Ruby's name represents connotes passion, which foreshadows her intense desire for romantic intimacy, and this desire is the instigator of her misdeeds. Ruby has allegedly murdered her first husband in addition to initiating numerous paranormal conspiracies against women whom she perceives as a threat to her romantic relationships. Ruby's fat is then emblematic of not just her outstanding talent but her abundant greed—her large size is an indicator of the difficulty she has with letting go and an illustration of how her romantic greed has become a burden to her. Additionally, her size has limited her perspective on life, and she is unable to maintain a broad focus. Ruby's eyes have become "pressed into tiny slits" because of her tremendous body, an indication of the myopia that has ensued. Her myopic tendencies specifically manifest as a relentless jealous obsession with her lover, Junior Lee (134).

Ruby's iconographic role as Big Mamma certainly goes awry, and this dysfunction reaches its zenith when she tries to murder Cocoa, Mama Day's niece. Ruby mistakenly suspects that Cocoa is interested in Junior Lee, and in response, Ruby attempts to poison Cocoa while braiding Cocoa's hair by incorporating nightshade into a batch of homemade hair oil.[37] Moreover, Ruby's choice of circumstances under which to commit her misdeed bears an intimate connection to her role as a dysfunctional Big Mamma. The hair-combing ritual has bonded black women for generations, and as Ruby invites Cocoa to take the traditional hair-braiding seat between Ruby's legs, Ruby's maternal role is indisputably enacted (245). Cocoa and Ruby's physical positions form a striking birthing image, and Cocoa's expectation that Ruby will provide the solace and encouragement associated with a Big Mamma's presumed surplus value of comfort is signified by Cocoa's perception of Ruby's legs as "a fortress I could hide between" (245). When Ruby braids Cocoa's hair with the poisonous oil, she dishonors a maternal gesture, transforming it into an acrimonious act of selfishness and fear and defiling her potential status as a Big Mamma.[38]

Despite Ruby's dysfunction as a maternal image, her large body nevertheless signifies abundance. Accumulating supernatural expertise equates to accumulating wealth because from the perspective of the disenfranchised, becoming wealthy is often perceived in the same register as performing magic. Because of this magical prowess, women like Ruby in *Mama Day* function as a kind of anti-colonial currency. When Ruby manipulates her environment to serve her she is mimicking the gestures of the hegemonic forces that marginalize her and the residents of Willow Springs based on race. Hence while Ruby might use her magic to harm, just possessing that magic signals a measure of resistance. Moreover, Ruby's paranormal powers are legendary, and Mama Day's benevolence indicates Ruby's potential as a source of healing and comfort for the residents of Willow Springs.[39] Mama Day consistently shares her knowledge of alternative medicine and her outstanding supernatural gifts with the community. As a foil for Mama Day, Ruby shows the consequence of misusing surplus value for private gain.[40]

Sofia Butler, one of the central characters in Alice Walker's *The Color Purple*, is not magically talented, but her large body is associated with resourcefulness and an abundance of self-determination. Her function as anti-colonial currency rests primarily with her assertion of female independence symbolized by her fat body. Given the historically masculinized nature of the colonial forces that subjugate Sofia, her very gendered independence represents her anti-colonial function as an aggressive agent against the masculine strains of colonialism.

Sofia's body is a mirror of her strength, and Celie, narrator of Walker's epistolary novel, describes Sofia as "strong and ruddy looking, like her mama brought her up on pork" (32). From our initial introduction to Sofia, it becomes apparent that her surplus value is defined by her stubbornness and emotional independence. After becoming pregnant for her boyfriend Harpo, she visits with him and his father, Mister, for the first time. Mister is the walking embodiment of misogyny and challenges Sofia's chastity, implying that perhaps Harpo is not the father of the child Sofia is carrying and that she wants to marry Harpo because her father threw her out of his house (32). Unruffled by Mister's allegations and recognizing that Harpo is afraid of his father, Sofia departs, invoking Harpo's own dependence on his father against the backdrop of her freedom: "I ain't living in the street. I'm living with my sister and her husband. They say I can live with them for the rest of my life," Sofia explains (33). "Well, nice visiting. I'm going home," she bids Mister farewell (33). But when Harpo rises to leave with her, she objects, "Naw, Harpo, you stay here. When you free, me and the baby be waiting" (33).

The fleshy female body is the literal and metaphoric source of Sofia's economic independence from both her father and Harpo. She is very close to her five sisters, who are described as "big strong healthy girls" who "look like amazons" (71). These sisters are a refuge for Sofia, taking her in when their father disowns her, supporting her throughout her marriage, and finally helping move her from Harpo's house when the relationship completely disintegrates (71). The noise from the sisters' movements as they help Sofia pack symbolizes the collective forcefulness of the fat female body: "All us hear from inside is the thump, thump, thump of plump and stout feet. As Sofia sisters moving around together at one time make the house shake" (72). The sisters are a collective version of Big Mamma, their unity destabilizing to the patriarchal power structure and literalized as a "shake up" of Sofia's home.[41] Quite importantly, the house has a distinctly paternal heritage and is passed down from Mister's father to Harpo (35).

Before the complete collapse of Sofia and Harpo's marriage, their relationship is continually affected by Sofia's forceful determination: "I tell her to do one thing," Harpo complains, and "she do another" (37).

Advised by both his father and Celie to beat Sofia into submission, Harpo ends up severely bruised after engaging Sofia in a fight (38). Eventually the couple begins to settle into non-traditional domestic roles, Sofia often working in the field and doing repairs to the house while Harpo cooks and cares for their children; however, Harpo is never completely satisfied with the power dynamics of the marriage, and at one stage he competes for dominance by trying to gain weight and acquire a large body like Sofia's: "Food on his mind morning, noon and night. His belly grow and grow, but the rest of him don't," Celie explains (64). Harpo's weight-gain only results in making him look pregnant, further entrenching him in the feminine sphere he wishes to resist.

During Harpo and Sofia's separation, her stubborn and rebellious behavior does not abate, and when she defies the white political power structure, she encounters tremendous retaliation. One day the Mayor's wife approaches Sofia, admiring her children's cleanliness and enquiring if Sofia would like to be her maid (90). "Hell no," Sofia answers, causing a row between her and the mayor, with whom she ends up in a fist fight (90). Subsequently, the court sentences her to jail for twelve years, and she spends part of that time working for the Mayor's family as a domestic. This experience severely damages Sofia both physically and emotionally, but although these hegemonic efforts effect her submission, she nevertheless emerges as an icon of emotional resources within the mayor's family. When the mayor purchases a car for his wife but refuses to teach her how to drive, the wife ends up relying on Sofia for driving lessons (107–8). Additionally, Sofia bonds with the mayor's daughter, and even after the girl becomes an adult, she seeks out Sofia to help alleviate family disputes (210).

While Sofia never acquires any significant wealth, her fleshy body consistently reinforces her abundance of self-will and determination.[42] Interestingly, Oprah played the role of Sofia in the film version of *The Color Purple,* a role for which she was ideally suited because of her own large body at that time.[43] Oprah's body usually appears as either a fat body or a slender to average-sized body struggling against fatness, and although her often copious figure is an apt representation of her flourishing financial health, her body's interaction with the public has been marked by a perpetual struggle with her weight. Oprah's body is, then, an important site for the representational conflict between her oppressive racial history (assuaged by her large body) and her monetary wealth. However, Oprah's body is simultaneously responding to a more recent gendered oppression that makes unrealistic aesthetic demands of the female body, and she represents herself as consistently struggling to either become or remain slender.

Oprah once identified a diet that resulted in significant weight loss as the epitome of her achievements, raising the question of how this accomplishment could compare to her astronomical financial and professional success. Perhaps this is an appropriate place to recognize an intersection between Oprah's life and Sofia's life. Just as Sofia was literally beaten into submission, Oprah's self-perception has been perpetually pummeled by regiments from America's beauty police, whose job it is to ensure unwavering dedication to the beauty aesthetic of the dominant white cultural majority. Despite her extraordinary financial success, she has not prevailed in this battle, and both Oprah and Sofia enjoy the disconcerting spoils of submission.

In Derek Walcott's epic *Omeros*, yet another large black woman features as a central character. Ma Kilman is the *sorciere* or obeah woman of her village, and unlike Sofia, her activities are far less constrained due to race and gender. This freedom allows her to function in a healing and reconciliatory role for her entire community, much like Mama Day. Ma Kilman's corpulence is associated with both her economic status and her outstanding paranormal talent; moreover, she embodies resistance to hegemonic forces through her communal acts of healing wounds created by the Caribbean's colonial heritage.[44]

Although *Omeros* is set in the Caribbean, the portrayal of Ma Kilman's large body as a source of supernatural abundance is very similar to other portrayals across the Diaspora, namely Madame Koto in *The Famished Road* and Ruby in *Mama Day*. All these texts share the characteristic of having the black woman's fleshy body as the venue for an extraordinary accumulation of magical powers. This aesthetic similarity arises from the shared historical and cultural legacy of the African Diaspora and from the interrelatedness of the postcolonial trauma addressed by these fat bodies.[45] Furthermore, as a male author, Walcott's aesthetic treatment of Ma Kilman does not appear significantly different from the treatment of other large female characters by diasporic women writers. Walcott's proclivity for literary mimicry perhaps accounts for this consistency since his narrative strategy is anchored in a framework more significantly impacted by its nationalist agenda than any gender-specific motives.

A twentieth-century Caribbean fishing village where Ma Kilman operates the No Pain Café is the primary site for the re-enactment of the colonial trauma that Ma Kilman assuages. She is described as a "generously featured" woman, and this generosity is also a hallmark of her business, which offers comfort and protection as did the lodging houses of Ma Kilman's historical predecessors Mary Seacole and Rachel Pringle (243). The No Pain Café serves numerous functions, and among other things, it is a rum bar frequented by villagers seeking a leisurely escape. It is also the central gathering place for the fishermen, and nighttime street festivities seem to center around the bar. Furthermore, the café is a grocery store, supplying the villagers with a range of goods from food items to hurricane supplies.

The words used to portray Ma Kilman's expansive body connote her position as someone who serves the community. Of the three times that her size is described, she is once referred to as "large" (245) and twice using the term "generous" as a descriptor of her physical features (243, 273). The latter terminology suggests an implicit link between her girth and her magnanimity, coding Ma Kilman's excess weight as a sort of communal surplus value that she willingly shares with those around her.[46] Additionally, Ma Kilman's name and social status relate to her communal service, establishing that her detachment from the patriarchal order facilitates her generosity. "Kil[l] man" unabashedly implies her ability to resist patriarchal forces, if not a compulsion to do so. She is not merely a fighter or someone who is courageous in the face of masculine oppression; she is an independent, assertive, and aggressive agent who will annihilate the source of her subjugation. Furthermore, her status as a childless widow relieves Ma Kilman from the traditional expectations of female domesticity.

Ma Kilman's mystical posture is well received by her community, and she utilizes her powers to help those in need. For example, she is able to channel the deceased wife of Major Plunkett, a British expatriate who lives on the island (306). The text also intimates that she is in contact with her own deceased husband, who helped name her shop the No Pain Café as his personal "prophecy" about life after death (17). Furthermore, she provides medical care for the community through her knowledge of bush medicine. But the most significant use of her magical capabilities involves healing Philoctete, a local fisherman.

The rusty anchor of a ship cuts Philoctete on his leg, and his wound is unable to heal. His ailment represents the agony of the Caribbean's colonial trauma and the pain endured by those who have inherited this history of subjugation. The anchor is a vivid symbol of the malevolent slave trade since it is associated with both the Middle Passage as well as the metaphorical weight of the attendant oppression of slavery. Additionally, Philoctete's sore is imbued with a divine aura when he is described as "anoint[ing]" it, rendering the wound as parallel to Christ's wounds, which were also anointed (18).

Philoctete not only links his wounds to the divine but also to history because he believes his injury has come from the chains that shackled his forefathers' feet, and the poem correlates current aspects of Philoctete's experience to the historical trauma in which his wound is grounded (19). The collective quality of this trauma is further represented when school children taunt Philoctete and mispronounce his name "Pheelosophee" (19). Philoctete's predicament then takes on "philosophical" implications, which suggest that his wound provides a paradigm to help negotiate the psychical ground of postcolonial territory.

Ma Kilman tries to assist Philoctete as she does many of the other villagers, but she is unsuccessful in finding a cure for his injury. As Philoctete approaches her bar, she sets out her various medicines for him: Vaseline, a basin of ice, and a flask of rum (18). The failure of these treatments may also be rooted in their connection to the island's colonial legacy, especially since rum is a by-product of sugar production, an industry that epitomizes the ravages of slavery. The Vaseline is also a by-product, but in this case of the petroleum industry, and its artificiality signals a clear disconnection from natural remedies. Finally, ice is explicitly associated with northern climates, the geographic terrain of colonial forces of oppression. In addition to providing these remedies, Ma Kilman advises Philoctete to rest, but none of these curatives heal the wound, and she tries to remember which plant she saw her grandmother use to treat similar injuries. One day after church, Ma Kilman sets off through the woods on a quest to find this mysterious plant.

To get into the forest she follows a goat trail, and her body must then become agile like a goat's, as she maneuvers between trees and rocks (238). This metamorphosis imagery is further supported during the hillside ritual she uses to help her discern the healing plant, and she makes a goat's bleating sound (244). Additionally, during this ceremony a proliferation of ants crawl in and out of her hair, and when Ma Kilman comes to understand their language, they release the identification of the secret plant; this interpretative ability again connotes that her fleshy body is a locus for transformative opportunities (244).

Eventually Ma Kilman finds the healing plant and administers it to Philoctete through a medicinal bath. She bathes him in a vat from an old sugar plantation, another image that evokes the colonial past that she opposes. Once her brew is ready, she puts Philoctete in the potion to soak away his pain and the community's collective agony. In the act of bathing him she assumes a maternal posture, but she also takes on the role of sexual aggressor and his behavior is feminized through his anxiety and timidity as he trembles when she leads him to the vat (247). Once the brew begins to work and Philoctete, who is fearful, tries to make a premature departure from the tub, Ma Kilman intercepts his escape and "rams" him back into position, telling him it is not over as yet (247). The verb "rammed" intimates aggressive sexual behavior, and telling him to wait a bit longer adds to this sexual trope by suggesting orgasmic anticipation. In this scene Ma Kilman's function bifurcates into both a maternally and sexually constructed definition, challenging the often dichotomized roles of mother and sexual entity (247).

Ma Kilman's success with finding the correct plant to heal Philoctete is related to her ability to see, and there are several references to Ma Kilman's sight and specifically her spectacles. They are repeatedly described as being "cracked," implying that her view of the world is filtered through a medium that offers a different perspective and suggesting the need for us to reconsider the interpretive mechanisms that we use to understand our environment and the need to embrace non-traditional ways of seeing (306–7). By extension, this suggestion certainly implicates the inheritance of Western beauty culture as an infraction against the Caribbean since it diminishes the aesthetic viability of fat bodies like Ma Kilman's.

However, in response to this diminishment, Ma Kilman's large body foreshadows her enormous psychic and healing powers and relates to the enormity of the colonial fissures she is expected to assuage. Her body signals the recovery of the Caribbean's stolen surplus value, which she redistributes through her benevolent acts of social service. Like the Caribbean higgler, Ma Kilman's fat is emblematic of her resourcefulness, an essential component of her anti-colonial strategy. Ma Kilman's fat black female body is a site of recovery and resonates with the trauma of Caribbean history as well as the essence of that history's redemption.

Pockets of silence riddle Caribbean history, and it is not insignificant that the corporeality of the large black woman's body stands in stark opposition to these absences. Mimi Sheller suggests that there is an "exclusion of the Caribbean from the imagined time-space of Western modernity," and in her study, *Consuming the Caribbean*, she interrogates the impact of this "symbolic exclusion" on our conceptualization of the modern West (1).[47] Moreover, Sheller situates this exclusion as a form of consumption, marked by selective historical evictions and the general absorption of Caribbean objects and culture into the Western gut. It is against this cannibalistic backdrop that the fat black woman's body functions as a form of "cultural capital," which resists the Caribbean's legacy of being consumed.[48] Her fat body is the site of this resistance, powerfully signifying the Caribbean's ability to consume and to resist becoming the object of consumption.

While this image of corpulence presents a number of symbolic complications, namely the association of the large body with capitalistic excess and greed, the fat black woman nevertheless continues to occupy a unique psychic space in the literary imagination. Her body responds to the numerous sites of deprivation and economic oppression throughout the Diaspora and is often a metaphor for paranormal and material abundance. Some forms of fascination with and focus upon the fat black female body aim to detract from the Diaspora's legacy of racism and economic oppression. Cargill's marvel at how the higgler's body is able to become so large as well as the mystification of African American women's domestic skills, are both tactics that seek to disengage our attention from the socioeconomic contexts that have produced the higgler and the African American domestic. While the fleshy black female body may not contribute to any logistical resolution to slavery's racist legacy, its literary and cultural treatment does at the very least reveal some of the intricate psychic associations that have evolved among corpulence, blackness, and gender.

NOTES

1. Women's increasing fixation on becoming slender suggests a subconscious rejection of their femininity as well as reproductive capacity in exchange for professional mobility. The current body image trend of attaining both a slender and taut body implies a concomitant privileging of masculinity. Moreover, there is a physiological connection between slenderness and fertility. In her landmark study, Rose Frisch asserts that fat is a crucial precursor of fertility, and the lack of sufficient body fat can delay the onset of menstruation and diminish a woman's fertility. This potential delay in female maturation due to insufficient body fat further underscores the rejection of fat as a rejection of the maternal function. See Rose Frisch, *Female Fertility and the Body Fat Connection* (Chicago: University of Chicago Press, 2002).

2. Laura Fraser, *Losing It: America's Obsession with Weight and the Industry That Feeds on It* (New York: Dutton Books, 1997), 8. Fraser estimates that Americans may spend as much as $50 billion per year on diet products. Her estimate includes the traditionally quoted expenditures on items such as diet sodas, fitness club memberships, commercial diet plans, and appetite suppressants. Additionally, she takes the money spent on weight reduction surgeries and pharmaceutical diet aids into consideration.

3. Meg Richards, "Bill Gates Still Leads Billionaires' List," *Information Week* (March 1, 2003). In 2003 Oprah Winfrey became the first black woman on Forbes magazine's list of billionaires. At the time she had net worth of one billion.

4. James Ferguson, *The Story of the Caribbean People* (Kingston: Ian Randle Publishers, 1999), 106–7.

5. Kenneth F. Kiple and Virginia H. Kiple, "Deficiency Diseases in the Caribbean," *Caribbean Slavery in the Atlantic World*, eds. Verene Shepherd and Hilary McD. Beckles (Kingston: Ian Randle Publishers, 2000), 788.

6. Dorothy Schneider and Carl J. Schneider, *Slavery in America: From Colonial Times to the Civil War* (New York: Facts on File, 2000), 83.

7. Schneider and Schneider, *Slavery in America*, 83.

8. James Gray et al., "The Prevalence of Bulimia in a Black College Population," *International Journal of Eating Disorders* 7 (1988): 733–40; L. K. George Hsu, "Are the Eating Disorders Becoming More Common among Blacks?" *International Journal of Eating Disorders* 7 (1988): 113–24; Doris Witt, *Black Hunger: Food and the Politics of U.S. Identity* (New York: Oxford University Press, 1999), 186–87. Witt suggests that the exclusion of African American women from eating disorder discourses is intentional (although perhaps subconscious) and comprises a "constitutive absence" (187). I believe this absence underscores assumptions of black female appetite (like the black female body) as unruly and out of control in contrast to the Euro-feminine ideal of restraint.

9. "The Body of the Beholder," *Newsweek* 125, no. 7 (April 24, 1995): 66, Expanded Academic ASAP, Infotrac, University of Miami, accessed January 7, 2004 <http://web3.infotrac.galegroup.com>.

10. Karl Marx, *Capital: A Critique of Political Economy*, trans. Samuel Moore and Edward Aveling, ed. Frederick Engels (New York: The Modern Library, 1906).

11. Marx, *Capital*, 235.

12. See my discussion of Tsitsi Dangarembga's *Nervous Conditions* in chapter one and my discussion of Okot p'Bitek's "Song of Lawino" in the conclusion.

13. *Monday's Girls*, directed by Ngozi Onwyrah. Videocassette. California Newsreel, 1994.

14. Pat Lowery Collins, *The Fattening Hut* (Boston: Houghton Mifflin, 2003).

15. Garine, Igor De and Georgius J. A. Koppert, "Guru-Fattening Sessions among the Massa," *Ecology of Food and Nutrition* 25 (1991): 1–28. Furthermore, the Massa tribe of Chad and Northern Cameroon hold male fattening sessions.

16. Although one might argue that the fattening of the woman is ultimately for male pleasure, women at least attain the temporary benefit of relatively lavish care.

17. Both Pringle and Seacole were of mixed ancestry (African and European), and historical evidence suggests that their racial status was the central reason why they had access to their entrepreneurial opportunities. See Pedro L. V. Welch, "'Unhappy and Afflicted Women?': Free Colored Women in Barbados: 1780–1834," *Revista/Review Interamericana* 29 (1999), Inter American University of Puerto Rico, accessed Jan. 30, 2004, <www.sg.inter.edu/revista-ciscla/volume29/welsh.html>. Also see Paulette A. Kerr, "Victims or Strategists? Female Lodging-house Keepers in Jamaica," *Engendering History: Caribbean Women in Historical Perspective*, eds. Verene Shepherd, Bridget Brereton and Barbara Bailey (Kingston: Ian Randle Publishers, 1995), 197–212.

18. Welch, "'Unhappy and Afflicted Women?'"

19. Jerome Handler, "Joseph Rachel and Rachael Pringle-Polgreen: Petty Entrepreneurs," *Struggle and Survival in Colonial America*, eds. David G. Sweet and Gary B. Nash (Berkeley: University of California Press, 1981), 383.

20. Handler, "Joseph Rachel and Rachael Pringle-Polgreen," 383–84.

21. Handler, "Joseph Rachel and Rachael Pringle-Polgreen," 384.

22. Welch, "'Unhappy and Afflicted Women?'"

23. Seacole's image appears on a number of websites, including the following: *The Mary Seacole Centre for Nursing Practices*, The Faculty of Health and Human Sciences TVU, accessed April 1, 2004, <www.maryseacole.com/maryseacole/>; *1857—Mary Seacole—The Black Nurse*, Brighton and Hove Black History, accessed April 1, 2004, <www.black-history.org.uk/seacole.asp>.

24. Mary Seacole, *The Wonderful Adventures of Mrs. Seacole in Many Lands* (New York: Oxford University Press, 1988).

25. Seacole, *The Wonderful Adventures of Mrs. Seacole*, 197–99. Seacole became bankrupt as a result of her expenses during the war; however, several supporters aware of her outstanding efforts helped raise money on her behalf.

26. Seacole, *The Wonderful Adventures of Mrs. Seacole*, 81.

27. Franklin W. Knight, *The Caribbean: A Genesis of a Fragmented Nationalism* (Oxford: Oxford University Press, 1990), 136.

28. Knight, *The Caribbean*, 136; Sidney Mintz and Douglas Hall, "The Origins of the Jamaican Internal Marketing System," *Caribbean Slavery in the Atlantic World*, eds. Verene Shepherd and Hilary McD. Beckles (Kingston: Ian Randle Publishers, 2000), 758–73. See Mintz and Hall for a detailed discussion of the circumstances that created the Jamaican slave economy.

29. Hilary McD. Beckles, *Centering Woman: Gender Discourses in Slave Society* (Kingston: Ian Randle Publishers, 1999), 142.

30. Beckles, *Centering Woman*, 141.

31. Beckles, *Centering Woman*, 143.

32. Carla Freeman, "Is Local: Global as Feminine: Masculine? Rethinking the Gender of Globalization," *Signs* 26, no. 4 (Summer 2001), Expanded Academic ASAP, Infotrac, University of Miami, accessed January 7, 2004, <http://web3.infotrac.galegroup.com>. The phenomenon of women participating in transnational informal trade is not limited to the Caribbean and occurs in other third-world regions such as Africa and Latin America.

33. Lorna Goodison, "Bella Makes Life," *Baby Mother and the King of Sword* (Essex: Longman, 1990), 75–84. See Goodison's amusing short story for a literary characterization which merges higglering with the fat female body as the character Bella—a large Jamaican woman who travels to New York, where she becomes even larger, her fat body a naturalization of her increasing material acquisitions. Each time Bella returns home, she arrives with her huge suitcases full of "foreign" merchandise, which she sells to her customers on the island. The story situates America as a transformative site: the source of Bella's broadening body, her new outlandish taste in fashion, and her growing wealth. However, in exchange for these opportunities of accelerated financial growth, Bella becomes estranged from her husband, signaling a decreased engagement with Jamaican culture.

34. Morris Cargill, *Public Disturbances: A Collection of Writings 1986–1996* (Kingston: The Mill Press Ltd., 1998), 28–30.

35. Cargill's assumed homogeneity of the higgler is misguided. I have known several "uptown" Jamaican women who engage in higglering either as a full-time occupation or a part-time means of earning extra cash. Furthermore, Carla Freeman discusses the heterogeneity among Barbadian suitcase traders, identifying a clan of women who have professional positions but engage in higglering excursions for vacation pleasure as well as economic gain.

36. Gina Ulysse, "Uptown Ladies and Downtown Women: Informal Commercial Importing and the Social/Symbolic Politics of Identities in Jamaica," Ph.D. dissertation, University of Michigan, 1999.

37. Lindsey Tucker, "Recovering the Conjure Woman: Texts and Contexts in Gloria Naylor's *Mama Day*," *The Critical Response to Gloria Naylor*, eds. Sharon Felton and Michelle C. Loris (Westport, Conn.: Greenwood Press, 1997), 143–58. Tucker notes that Naylor's treatment of conjuring seeks to "de-mystify" this practice by making the reader aware that Cocoa is in fact poisoned and not under a magical spell of sorts.

38. Larry Andrews, "Black Sisterhood in Gloria Naylor's Novels," *College Language Association Journal* 33, no. 1 (Sept. 1989): 1–25. Andrews further explains the bonds that Ruby dishonors: "In Mama Day the power comes from folk tradition, from 'foremothering,' and from nature, as Naylor moves into the realm of

matriarchal mythmaking. At its best this bond among women confers identity, purpose, and strength for survival.

39. In the article "'The Only Voice Is Your Own': Gloria Naylor's Revision of *The Tempest*," Gary Storhoff considers *Mama Day* a revision of Shakespeare's *The Tempest*. He asserts that Mama Day (Miranda) is an inverted configuration of Prospero and his daughter Miranda and he points to her magical skill as evidence; however, he suggests that, in contrast to Prospero, Mama Day "consistently cooperates with natural forces" and is associated with "the Life Force" and not destruction, using her ongoing association with eggs and chickens (37). Gary Storhoff, "'The Only Voice Is Your Own': Gloria Naylor's Revision of *The Tempest*," *African American Review* 29, no. 1 (Spring 1995): 35–45.

40. See Ben Okri, *The Famished Road* (New York: Anchor Books, 1993). Set in Nigeria, Okri's novel also features a large black woman who misuses her magical talent and is perched at the border between the abstract and the real. Madame Koto owns and operates a bar that is situated on the edge of a forest, a site the novel associates with forays into the spiritual realm. Like the Oracle, Madame Koto is caretaker of this psychic junction between the pre-colonial world of spirits and the ever-encroaching and very real postcolonial realm of economic oppression. She is an abundant source of redress for her community, intervening to provide her assistance at times of crisis, especially in the life of the novel's main character, Azaro. Furthermore, Madame Koto follows Seacole and Pringle's path by earning a living in the hospitality arena, her wealth, generosity and supernatural talent conflated with her culinary skill, which is evident in her tasty homemade soup and palm wine. Madame Koto eventually turns to the dark side of her magic when she becomes involved with Nigeria's burgeoning political parties; however, like Ruby, the signifying power of her large body supercedes her poor moral choices as Madame Koto becomes even more powerful and wealthy.

41. Charles Heglar, "Named and Namelessness: Alice Walker's Pattern of Surnames in *The Color Purple*," *ANQ* 13, no. 1 (Winter 2000), 38, Expanded Academic ASAP, Infotrac, University of Miami, accessed July 14, 2004, <http://web3.infotrac.galegroup.com>. Heglar points out that in *The Color Purple*, Walker often does not give surnames to her male characters. For example, Sofia's brother-in-law is known only as "Jack" or "Odessa's husband" (Walker 153). Heglar explains that this narrative strategy "diminishes their patriarchal authority as, in contrast, supplying women's surnames establishes an alternative to male domination."

42. Harpo and Sofia's home, which is strongly associated with her persona as she did a great deal of labor to renovate the structure, eventually becomes the location of Harpo's successful juke-joint. While Sofia does not operate this business, its financial success further implies Sofia's resourcefulness.

43. *The Color Purple*, directed by Steven Spielberg, starring Whoopi Goldberg and Oprah Winfrey, Warner Bros., 1985.

44. Loretta Collins, "'We Shall All Heal': Ma Kilman, The Obeah Woman, as Mother-Healer in Derek Walcott's *Omeros*," *Literature and Medicine* 14, no. 1 (1995): 146–62. According to Collins, "As a magic-spiritual means of altering economic, biological, or socio-cultural relations, obeah is an ideal medium for the cultural, historical, and individual healing in *Omeros*" (147).

45. Collins also suggests that Ma Kilman "recalls the rage, guilt, and fears of the long tradition of colonial oppression, yet she also recalls an essential connection to ancestral communities and mother-culture" (150).

46. Julie A. Minkler, "Helen's Calibans: A Study of Gender Hierarchy in Derek Walcott's *Omeros*," *World Literature Today* 67, no. 2 (Spring 1993): 272–76. Ma Kilman's large body also connotes her maternal nature and Minkler suggests that she "represents the domesticated version of Sycorax, Caliban's absent mother" (273).

47. Mimi Sheller, *Consuming the Caribbean* (London: Routledge, 2003).

48. Stuart Hall, "What is this 'Black' in Black Popular Culture? (Rethinking Race)," *Social Justice* 20, nos. 1–2 (Spring–Summer 1993): Expanded Academic ASAP, Infotrac, University of Miami, accessed March 28, 2004, <http://web3.infotrac.galegroup.com>. In this essay, Hall develops the concept of the black woman's body as "cultural capital."

4

Spectacles of Size

The Performing Bodies of Fat Black Women

Despite the conspicuous marginalization of the fat black woman's body in the American beauty arena, there is a curious abundance of these bodies on the musical performance stage. In fact, the popularity of fat black female singers suggests that a privileged performative space exists for them while it does not exist for their large white counterparts. There are few famous, full-figured white women on the contemporary landscape of American popular music, and among the couple who come to mind are Carnie Wilson, who has lost a considerable amount of weight and can hardly count as fat anymore, and Wynonna Judd, whose weight battles are frequent tabloid news. The international scope of the anxieties about body size and white femininity is substantiated by some of the incidents that have made the news as supposedly "large" white women either try to enter or to maintain their place in the entertainment industry.

In England, controversy struck when Michelle McManus, a robust Scottish woman, was voted the British Pop Idol for 2003. Because of her size the British public engaged in an extensive debate over her viability as a celebrity; in fact, one Pop Idol judge went as far as storming off the set of the show when McManus' victory was announced in December, 2003.[1] He proclaimed McManus' win to be "rubbish," an indication of his disgust over her large body infringing on territory usually reserved for the likes of Britney Spears and Jessica Simpson.[2] The Royal Opera House in London did not shy away from its opportunity to incite further fat controversy when it fired leading soprano Deborah Voigt. Weighing a reported 250 pounds, Voight was dismissed because she could not fit into the costume for her lead role in an opera.[3]

In contrast to these anxieties about the public exposure of white women's large bodies, American popular culture has a lengthy history of embracing fat black female performers. From blues divas such as Ma Rainey and Bessie Smith, to Aretha Franklin and Jennifer Holliday, and more recently women like Queen Latifah, Angie Stone, Missy Elliott, and Jill Scott, full-bodied black women have managed to parlay their talents into extremely successful careers despite America's racism, sexism and white-inflected gender norms. While a few of these performers, like Ma Rainey and Bessie Smith, gained success by initially catering to a black audience, the modern-day diva Jill Scott has had to struggle to get her music played on black radio since some station managers presume her neo-soul sound to be more of a white commodity.[4] Whether firmly situated in one racial market or the other, or transcending the borders of multiple entertainment niches, large black women have attained measurable success in the music industry.

When Bessie Smith released her first record in 1923, it was among the earliest records by an African American artist, and within a year she had sold over one million copies.[5] Fast forward to the end of the twentieth century: Angie Stone's debut album, *Black Diamond*, goes platinum, she wins two Lady of Soul awards and is nominated for a Grammy.[6] Jill Scott's debut album, *Who Is Jill Scott?*, also goes platinum and she receives three Grammy nominations.[7] Missy Elliott, reigning queen of rap, releases five albums in only six years, earns two Grammys, the 2003 American Music Award, and MTV's 2003 Video of the Year.[8] Additionally, Missy garners a number of corporate endorsement deals with companies such as Coca-Cola and Gap.[9] Queen Latifah becomes both a best-selling recording artist and an Oscar nominee with a long list of movies in her filmography.[10] She also owns and directs an entertainment management company that oversees the careers of several new talents on the music scene.[11] Additionally, Queen Latifah becomes a spokesperson for Cover Girl and along with Jill Scott appears on *People Magazine*'s prestigious list of America's fifty most beautiful people in 2003 and 2001 respectively.[12]

Given the fierce rivalry for opportunities in the musical entertainment industry, the level of competition becoming even more apparent with the advent of *American Idol*, why are these robust black women able to succeed in what certainly appears to be disproportionate numbers? What is the nature of the performative space that they inhabit, or rather how does it differ from the space afforded white women? The black woman's large body is particularly well-suited for the stage because of that body's transgressive and disruptive cultural significations. The stage has historically been a transgressive space, especially for women, for whom restrictions from public exposure have been a constant feature of sexism in the Americas.

The function of the fat black woman's body in the performative arena bears strong parallels to the role of hip-hop culture in America. Extensively embraced by white teens, hip-hop now dominates American youth culture.[13] Offering more than an opportunity to rebel against parents and the sociopolitical establishment, hip-hop provides an opportunity for its audience to partake in an "authentic" rebellion against actual social, economic and political oppression.[14] Hip-hop allows white and middle-class black teens, who sometimes have never experienced the debilitating impact of inner-city life (as is sometimes the case for the rappers themselves), to infuse their teenaged angst and upheaval with articulations of resistance to the very real circumstances of black marginalization. This infusion helps to authenticate and justify the adolescent anxieties of millions of young people, who do not live in the inner-cities. The large black bodies of female performers offer a parallel opportunity to the dominant white culture to engage in a relationship, whereby the unruliness attendant to both the bodies and performances of these women is simultaneously enjoyed by their audiences as a sociopolitical form of rebellion.[15] While some of America's large black women performers have varied in size over the course of their careers, this project is less concerned with them perpetually maintaining their full figure than with their ability to initiate or sustain a successful career with ample bodies.

This chapter initially engages all of the above issues within a North American context because the presence of competing white, and often slender, bodies further compels the question of why the American public accepts and in some ways identifies with these large black women. This public acceptance facilitates the opportunity for voluptuous divas to launch extremely successful careers despite the perpetual racist milieu in America and creates what appears to be a perplexing collision between racist hierarchies and popular sentiment. However, this chapter also discusses the performative presence of large black women in the Caribbean, including Trinidadian calypsonian Denise Belfon and Carlene the Jamaican dancehall queen.

All these women share the experience of rising to fame during the twentieth century, when technological advancements allowed their bodies to be in full focus of their respective cultures. Due to live or recorded concerts, album covers, newspaper advertisements, television appearances, and more recently music videos, it is increasingly difficult to separate the physicality of a performer from her performance. Indeed, talent competitions like *American Idol* have made it apparent that a singer's appearance competes with her musical talent for the role of being the primary component of her musical persona.[16] It is, perhaps, at a live performance that an audience becomes most aware of a performer's embodiment, and the transgressive nature of the stage is replicated in the corporeal qualities of the fat black woman.

The historical evolution of the North American theater industry reveals the stage's transgressive nature, in part because the stage provided a space to explore identity and creatively engage racial and gender anxieties. Race played a pivotal role in American live performances from as early as the 1840s when blackface minstrelsy began to develop, though it is worth noting that African Americans did not even participate in these highly racialized performances until the 1860s.[17] Minstrelsy eventually became the most popular form of American theater between the 1850s and the 1880s.[18] Minstrels, almost exclusively white and male, festooned themselves in carnivalesque costumes, darkened their faces and painted their lips as they transmogrified themselves and enacted white, masculine imaginings of blackness and femininity.[19]

According to Robert Toll, "minstrelsy seemed to have a magnetic, almost hypnotic, impact on its audiences," and this is no surprise given the outlandish nature of blackface performances (33).[20] Toll's description of one minstrel troupe, the Virginia Minstrels, indicates how this early form of American theater sustained its popularity through exorbitant and exaggerated constructions of blackness:

> [The Virginia Minstrels] burst on stage in makeup which gave the impression of huge eyes and gaping mouths. They dressed in ill-fitting, patchwork clothes, and spoke in heavy "nigger" dialects. Once on stage, they could not stay still for an instant. Even while sitting, they contorted their bodies, cocked their heads, rolled their eyes, and twisted their outstretched legs. When the music began, they exploded in a frenzy of grotesque and eccentric movements. (36)

While the historical popularity of this art form reveals white America's ongoing angst regarding race as well as its desire to enter into negotiations of the color line from taboo perspectives of otherness, it also suggests that race, gender and spectacle are tightly conjoined.

Live theater performance was an ongoing source of leisure in the U.S.A. well into the early nineteen hundreds, and between the 1880s and the 1920s it was the country's principal form of entertainment.[21] In the late eighteen hundreds, the role of women in theater began to change as some became comediennes instead of simply the butt of comedy.[22] In her study of women in American theater, Susan Glenn explains: "As an influential group of women in musical comedy and vaudeville challenged the assumption that comedy was a male domain, the right to be funny gained increasing cultural legitimacy" (41). In carving out a theatrical niche for themselves, female performers tended towards either end of a dichotomy: beautiful and dignified or unconventional and disruptive. The latter group of "newcomers in grotesqueries" became a nascent wave of female comics who "won their claims to fame by going overboard, violating gender norms through their excessiveness" (Glenn 45–46). The growth of this new feminized performative space for the "grotesque" allowed some women to become extremely popular entertainers; however, an intriguing component of their success related to the curious juxtaposition of body size and ethnicity.

Fat women's bodies were fertile ground for comedy routines, and at the turn of the nineteenth century, when imperatives of slenderness took hold in American culture, the fat female body became an intrinsic source of humor.[23] The major comediennes of that era included May Irwin, Fay Templeton, Trixie Friganza, and Marie Dressler, all fat white women who used their size as a basis for their humor.[24] Dressler, who was five foot seven and sometimes weighed as much as 220 pounds, would gracelessly trudge around the stage, stumbling into furniture, to elicit laughter from her audience.[25] Self-described as unattractive, Dressler believed her appearance contributed to her success as a comic.[26] Her clumsy stage persona sprang from efforts to approximate cultural expectations of inadequacy associated with fatness and ugliness. Just as minstrelsy provided a reflection of how the white collective consciousness perceived blackness, Dressler's unwieldy characters validated assumptions and assuaged anxieties regarding the unfeasibility of female fatness or homeliness as a legitimate state of feminine embodiment.

Friganza also responded to the cultural impulses to marginalize her ample body by anticipating social reaction to herself and negotiating the context of her marginalization on her own comedic terms. In her vaudeville performances she tackled size via an array of acts that dealt with the difficulties of a fat girl's experience.[27] She also had a routine in which a chorus line of girls performed ballet moves while Friganza awkwardly approximated their steps.[28] Like Dressler, Friganza helped sustain the notion of fat as an abnormal state of physicality, and she recognized the comic capital her large body provided as a means of rendering her disruptive. Friganza believed that audiences would not find slender women funny, undoubtedly because she was aware that their tiny bodies do not have the disruptive connotations fundamental to her comic enterprise.[29]

This requirement of "grotesquerie" and extreme for female comediennes, in fact for any female performer who did not qualify as traditionally pretty, leads to a unique interplay between size and race, and the experiences of white entertainer Sophie Tucker exemplifies how both these physiological features contributed to creating conflicted performative opportunities for women. In the early stages of her career, Tucker visited a theater to compete for a spot on the amateur night show. After being accepted she heard the theater manager instructing his assistant regarding her stage presentation: "This one's so big and ugly the crowd out front will razz her. Better get some cork and black her up. She'll kill 'em" (Tucker 33).[30] In the manager's estimation, Tucker's size and unattractive features were too unacceptable a combination to be staged as a marketable representation of white womanhood.

His response to "black her up" was based on his recognition that black femininity was one of the final frontiers of socially unacceptable womanhood, and thus Tucker could be acceptably incorporated under this rubric—this domain of the woman dispossessed of her femininity—without issue. History seems to exonerate him—not of his racism but of any doubts about his knowledge in the entertainment management industry since Tucker went on to have a successful career in which she was sometimes billed as a "Coon Shouter."[31] "Coon," a derogatory term for African Americans, came to denote a category of musical performances in which entertainers sang to a ragtime melody.[32] In addition to Tucker, many other performers sang "coon" songs as a component of their minstrelsy, including May Irwin, who performed a controversial song titled "All Coons Look Alike to Me" in an 1896 musical production.[33] Even the famous Lillian Russell included elements of black impersonation in her routines, specifically in the 1899 comedy burlesque *Whirl-i-Gig*, about which one review headline read "Lillian Russell Sings Coon Songs in New Burlesque" (Glenn 54).

The stage has traditionally been a space where people expect to be confronted with the spectacular—with outrageous behavior such as Russell's —and one of the primary components of the spectacular is that it crosses the boundaries of the normative. These border crossings occur as somewhat dichotomized possibilities. On one hand, a performer may cross the boundaries of the normative because she supercedes socially desirable criteria: for example, she may be extremely beautiful or her voice particularly outstanding. On the other hand, she may traverse those boundaries because she exceeds a socially *undesirable* standard: she is fat, black or unattractive. However, these categories are at times complicated by some degree of slippage as in Russell's case. She was beautiful and talented (although she gained weight as her career progressed), exceeding several desirable criteria for the normative, but with her minstrel-type performances she simultaneously crossed those borders of normativeness going in the opposite direction: into the realm of excess—blackness and hypersexuality. This made Russell a particularly attractive spectacle because during her "coon shouting" performances she embodied divergent realms of excess, teasing the American imagination's racial and gender norms through the metaphoric performance of miscegenation.

The popularity of minstrelsy in its various incarnations—the early blackface performances, Russell's "coon" shouting, Madonna's attempts to portray herself as racially ambivalent, and, more recently, Eminem's raps—indicates the potency of physiological blackness or enactments of blackness to render a performer more desirable for the stage. However, this rendering reflects the complicated nature of the stage as an expressive space because it is a locale that situates blackness as a form of deviance—an excess of the undesirable. The related association of black skin with hypersexuality and animalistic behavior has contributed to the long history of black-inflected performance strategies that render blackness an enduring state of spectacle.

Because of the cultural desirability associated with an excess of the undesirable, the American stage has historically made provisions for the inclusion of marginalized bodies—whether these bodies are authentically marginalized as in Tucker's case, or costumed to represent marginalized bodies, as in the case of white minstrels. Hence the performance stage incorporates a conflicting multi-level paradigm for judging aesthetic beauty, a paradigm that in some modalities reconfigures the popular culture's aesthetic standards. With regard to female identity, this reconfiguration recognizes the stage as a venue for both the showcasing of idealized womanhood—white, slender and conformist—or deviant femininity, which is often contextualized as absurd and consequently humorous. The stage is then one of the only public spaces that provides room for women to make a spectacle of themselves: Josephine Baker can expose her banana-clad body, or Madonna and Britney Spears can engage in a lustful, homoerotic kiss. Furthermore, the stage has been one of the few venues where women beyond the culture's aesthetic ideal, women who like Tucker were "too big and too ugly," could appear before the American public, resplendent in their awkwardness, and there they could garnish praise for their "inappropriate" appearance and behavior. Hence the stage is multifunctional, operating as both an entertainment showcase for idealized femininity as well as a transgressive space in which women can, at least temporarily, subvert gender norms.[34]

Because of this latter quality of the stage, fatness and blackness have been accepted and even encouraged as a performance aesthetic. It is from knowing that the stage thrives in part off the showcasing of undesirability that Friganza padded her already ample body, and Tucker blackened her face as a means of enhancing the nature of their transgressions against cultural norms of their time. This perspective on the stage is the key to answering this chapter's initial question of why fat black women have been able to achieve what seems like extraordinary success in the entertainment industry—particularly as singers. This accomplishment is especially noteworthy because they work in a profession where success is heavily dependent on appearance and in a culture where they are marginalized because of the physical characteristics of size, race and gender in most other arenas. Furthermore, their primary physiological characteristics all bear connotations of unruliness and disruption since blackness evokes licentiousness and femininity evokes historical undertones of hysteria. Finally, their fat bodies compound this notion of disorder and decadence by further suggesting a lack of control over food intake and hence a proclivity towards self-indulgence. Fat black women are, however, welcomed into performative spaces because of the transgressive qualities of these spaces and because the site of the fat black woman's body is in itself a source of social disruption and she is a poignant embodiment of transgression.

It is also necessary to discuss the fat black woman's performative status in terms of her audience's identification with her. The apparent conflict inherent in this notion, especially in relation to fat black women like Aretha Franklin and Queen Latifah, whose fans span America's racial and gender divide, has also been an issue that raises a number of questions. What creates that sense of connection between large divas and their fans—the slender Hispanic girl who loves Jill Scott, or the young white man who owns every Angie Stone album? The public's ability to identify with an entertainer has been established as part of the basis through which individuals become attracted to a celebrity.[35] Among other things, race and gender play a major role in determining celebrity identification, and one report suggests that black consumers have high levels of identification with black celebrity endorsers.[36] Assuming that white consumers similarly have high levels of identification with white celebrities further complicates the popularity of fat black women and compels the question of why fat black women's fan base does not exclusively consist of other fat black women.

Freud suggests that identification relies upon assumptions of similarity; furthermore, in his seminal text *The Interpretation of Dreams* he explains that identification has a component of envy and that inherent in identifying with someone is the desire to be in that person's place.[37] Based upon this component of Freud's identification theory, the next most obvious question arises: What do fat black women have that their audience want? Certainly the talent, fame and money concomitant with stardom must always be a source of envy, but what else? A turn-of-the-century newspaper article on Friganza tackled this question in light of her weight and concluded that audiences identified with Friganza's fat body because through this site they could vicariously break cultural taboos, specifically those relating to self-control.[38] In other words, fans metaphorically "envied" Friganza's fat because of its representational value as a form of cultural disobedience.

This notion of fat envy has informed this book's hermeneutics for reading the bodies of fat black women in the performative arena. These women embody heightened levels of unruliness because of their size *and* their race—two poignant sites of disruption to America's aesthetic ideal. Their fat, like Friganza's, represents a willingness to resist conformist pressures for slenderness and to indulge the body in culinary delight. Additionally, their black skin, loaded with significations including hypersexuality, registers another level of disobedience: an excessive indulgence of the body in sexual pleasures.[39] So when America gazes at large black women on the concert stage or listens to them on the radio, these women amuse beyond their performance by offering audiences an opportunity to pursue unfulfilled desire through a vicarious experience of embodying otherness through identification. Full-figured black women entertain America's collective yearning to free itself from imperatives of "appropriate" cultural conduct, and while their bodies may be aesthetically marginalized, they are at the center of American longing for release from inhibiting and restrictive cultural taboos, which are representatively embedded in the site of their black skin and fat bodies.[40]

Various elements of these large divas' entertainment persona, including their visual image, song lyrics and performance reviews, support the notion that both their bodies and performances mirror the transgressive qualities of the stage. The principal manifestation of their capacity for social disruption rests with their hypersexuality, which articulates itself in multiple forms. Perhaps primary expression of this hypersexuality is through the lyrical content of songs and by extension the musical genre in which many of these large black women have historically performed.

Rap, blues and other musical styles in the African Diaspora evolved from West Africa, where music was an expressive means of engaging a range of significant events, not only joyful celebrations like birth and marriage but emotionally challenging circumstances such as famine, war and death.[41] The slaves brought to the Americas from Africa participated extensively in this deployment of music as a therapeutic response to the ravages of slavery, and the blues is one of the earliest forms of that effort. With its origins in the American South, where it started as a form of black folk music, the blues combines the religious fervor of Negro spirituals with the uncoordinated spontaneity of field hollers—an impulsive musical rendering sung in a moaning fashion by black field hands.[42] This bluesian practice of using music to cope with the various oppressions of life, specifically black life, helps explain the dominance of large black women in this music genre. This outstanding number of full-bodied divas in the blues world includes Ma Rainey, Bessie Smith, Mamie Smith, June Richmond, Ida Cox, Ella Fitzgerald and Big Mama Thornton.

Black America's historical aesthetic appreciation for an ample figure helps explain this phenomenon but not sufficiently. While these large women enabled a vicarious subversion of cultural norms for both the black and white populace of the United States, their fatness functioned in specific ways within an African American context and marked them as metaphorical escapees from the racism of that period—their large bodies are associated with health and prosperity and hence disruptive to the hegemony's efforts to sustain black America's economic marginalization. This role as an agent of transgression against the white majority was an especially important one to a race of people submerged by America's Jim Crow laws and subjected to vicious acts of racist violence.[43] The blues evolved within this framework of oppression and has arguably been the most influential musical form in the history of American music. W. C. Handy, an accomplished African American musician, is known as "father of the blues" and sometimes credited as its originator.[44]

Blues diva Ma Rainey was a full-bodied performer who crafted an extravagant stage persona that symbolically corresponded to her large body. Dubbed "Mother of the Blues" by Paramount, her record company, Ma Rainey was the first black woman blues singer to rise to fame, and during the five years that she worked for Paramount, she made over ninety recordings.[45] She was known for her outlandish dress and often performed in outfits extravagantly decorated with rhinestones and sequins.[46] She festooned herself with flashy headdresses and horsehair wigs and had a weakness for elaborate jewelry.[47] Additionally, Ma had her makeup applied to lighten her dark features, and this ended up heightening her outlandish appearance as the powder and rouge made her seem yellow in the glow of the stage lighting.[48]

Furthermore, her full figure was prominently featured in promotions for her show and on album covers, which suggests that her girth was an important aspect of the spectacle she created.[49] One advertisement that appeared in the *Chicago Defender* bore the headline, "Dead Drunk Blues," and featured a cartoon drawing of Ma Rainey dancing and balancing her large body on top of a dining table where three black men are seated.[50] The men are dressed in formal suits and appear quite delighted with her performance as they sip from champagne glasses. The bucket of champagne is conspicuously placed in the forefront of the picture, situating the performance as an upper-class event, but even more importantly implying a demarcation between her and the patrons of her performance. The men's formal attire and financial access indicate middle to upper-class values and propriety, while Ma Rainey's comical dance suggests that her performance provides a carnivalesque escape for the patrons from middle-class behavioral norms. Furthermore, her position on top of their dining table implies that observing her performance is an act of consumption, an act rife with sexual undertones.

Early in her career Ma Rainey recognized the potency of the spectacular, and beyond the production of her elaborate entertainment persona, her shows were staged to astonish. In a 1914 performance in New Orleans she sang a popular number, and at a certain point in the song the stage came apart and caved in (Lieb 7). A 1926 newspaper review further indicates Ma Rainey's penchant for unusual stage antics as well as her popularity. The writer states: "Blues singers come and they go, but the way Ma draws them in she should be called the 'mother of packin' 'em in' along with her title of being the mother of the 'blues'" (Hayes 6).[51] During the same performance that the reviewer is discussing, he describes her grand entrance to the stage: "Ma Rainey is introduced. She is heard singing as only the mother of the 'blues' can sing, but unseen until she steps from a big Paramount talking machine. Oh boy! What a flash Ma does make in her gorgeous gowns" (Hayes 6). In addition to stage gimmicks, the words of Ma Rainey's songs and the musical style in which they were performed helped sustain her outrageous performance persona.

Ma Rainey wrote several of her songs, and she was considered one of the blues performers most firmly anchored in the folk music tradition from which the blues had sprung.[52] Her loyalty to her African American musical heritage must have rendered her a somewhat more "black" and hence genuine blues diva than her contemporaries such as Bessie Smith, whose style evolved away from its roots as her career progressed.[53] Ma Rainey's unwillingness to dilute her art form enhanced the racialized underscoring of her performance, and her black body performing historically black music must have imbued her with even more heightened levels of alterity and transgression. Her song lyrics also preserved her subversive persona. They covered a range of subjects, but the most popular theme was the passion and turmoil of intimate relationships.[54] Unlike most of the white female singers of her time, Ma Rainey sang of highly spirited women who were aware of their sexuality and aggressive in asserting their emotions.[55] In "Explaining the Blues" Ma Rainey tells the story of an abandoned woman whose man has left her because of her involvement with another man (Lieb 104). As in several of her songs, the protagonist in "Explaining the Blues" is quite a worldly woman who does not feel compelled to display any false modesty and who covertly indicates her comfort with the masculinized act of having concurrent intimate partners. In "Titanic Man Blues," co-written by Ma Rainey, the protagonist goes a step further and actually abandons her man for another (Lieb 110).[56] These direct sexual references and Ma Rainey's very frank engagement of the raw emotions attendant to romantic relationships aid in making her performances spectacular during an era when cultural norms discouraged female sexual agency.

In addition to Ma Rainey's overt engagement of sexuality in her songs, her off-stage life was also a source of sexual innuendo and transgression. Rumored to be bisexual, as was Bessie Smith, Ma Rainey developed a reputation as sexually aggressive towards younger men as well as actively involved in lesbian encounters.[57] During one incident Ma Rainey was arrested in Chicago after the police were called because of the noise she and a group of young women were making.[58] When the police arrived, Ma Rainey and her party were all undressed; she then tried to escape through the back door, but she had picked up the wrong dress.[59] One of Ma Rainey's band members even implied that she and Bessie Smith were lovers because Ma Rainey was quite protective of Bessie while the two toured together.[60] Ma Rainey's life and her sexual exploits may not have been that unusual, but what is significant is the extent to which her sexual activities have become an element of her historical legacy, further symbolizing her as disobedient.

Ma Rainey's extravagant dress and her fat body both complimented each other as agents of transgression.[61] Furthermore, her dark skin, broad face and flat nose challenged normative criteria for feminine beauty, and she even became known as "the ugliest woman in show business" (Bogle 21). The impact of Ma Rainey's fashion legacy on contemporary African American entertainers is apparent, and like her, many modern rap artists sport numerous gold fillings and garnish their bodies with a plethora of jewelry.[62] This connection helps shed light on how transgression continues to be a crucial constituent of success in modern performative arenas. It also illuminates the criticisms levied against rap stars for their outlandish dress and extravagant jewelry—affronts to mainstream *haute couture*—as a means of reinforcing class and social hierarchies and simultaneously re-inscribing African Americans as well as their cultural spaces as deviant. These modern fashion choices of rap performers are surely informed by the same cultural tensions that affected Ma Rainey that she manipulated for her professional success. This achievement was in part due to her recognition that the fat black woman's body was already an item of spectacle in American culture and that further embellishing that body to be more spectacular efficiently reinforced America's assumptions of blackness as deviance as well as America's desire to witness the astonishing.

Rhythm and blues queen Aretha Franklin has continued Ma Rainey's legacy by foregrounding women's sexuality and romantic heartache in her music. Daughter of a religious minister, Franklin began her singing career in the church, and she has released a number of gospel songs; however, she rose to fame in the 1960s with hits such as "Respect," "Natural Woman," and "I Never Loved a Man," which earned her the title, "Queen of Soul."[63] For most of her illustrious career, Aretha's passion-filled songs about relationships have often been delivered via her ample body. At one concert Aretha teased the audience, remarking that she managed her weight via a mixture of "Slim Fast and young men" (Franklin qtd. in Holden).[64]

This is an intriguing comment given Ma Rainey's history and suggests that Aretha recognizes the potency of her large body and black skin as a source of sexual transgression. In fact, she is aware of the need to market herself as a sexual transgressor/aggressor in order to attract and maintain her audience. This desire must surely be linked to Aretha's reputation for the tendency to overexpose herself, specifically her bust, through her revealing fashion choices. During the Clinton administration she performed in the Rose Garden, and for the event she wore an extremely low-cut dress, her large bosom forming high mounds above the dress's plunging neckline (Franklin 143).[65] In an essay exploring black female sexuality, critic bell hooks makes a similar observation as she comments on a PBS documentary featuring Aretha:

> throughout most of the documentary Aretha appears in what seems to be a household setting, a living room maybe, wearing a strapless evening dress, much too small for her breast size so her breasts appear like two balloons filled with water about to burst. (70)[66]

On yet another occasion Aretha's bust became the subject of controversy as she prepared to make a television appearance. The directors of *The Tonight Show* asked that she change her dress because it exposed too much cleavage; she refused, citing the novelty of her appearance—a black woman with huge breasts—as the show's real issue.[67] In other words, Aretha implied that the directors of *The Tonight Show* were unaccustomed to the spectacular potential of black female sexuality. Assuming that Aretha has some say in the manner her image is staged, her choice of revealing outfits for very public appearances suggests that she is trying to embellish the astonishing nature of her already highly eroticized persona.

While Aretha's background in the church might seem in contradiction with her inclination to overplay her sexuality, her gospel legacy and this impulse to over-eroticize herself actually cooperate in the structuring of an astonishing image. Gospel is renowned for its highly emotive style and its facility for expressing a divine variety of passion. It is not unusual to see gospel singers, especially in the black church, dance, sway, and pivot across the stage in frenzied movements that have strong sexual inflections and closely resemble an orgasmic climax. Aretha and other large black women such as Mahalia Jackson and CeCe Winans evoke this sensuality during their performances—even though with Jackson and Winans there might be far fewer sexual references. A major contributor to Aretha's success has been her ability to combine the divine and the erotic to create the spectacle of transformation through a musically framed sexual/spiritual encounter.

One performance where this amalgamation is particularly apparent is the "Divas Live" concert during which Aretha performs with some other pop music royalty, including Mariah Carey and Celine Dion.[68] Susan Sarandon introduces Aretha and summarizes her accomplishments in very reverent tones.[69] Sarandon speaks of Aretha being "anointed" queen of soul and describes her voice as a "beacon" that represents everyone (*Divas Live*).[70] Before Aretha even appears on stage Sarandon invokes the divine by shrouding her in religious imagery and situating her singing talents as akin to a divine capacity for ministering. For the finale Aretha appears dressed in a floor-length, black dress with a very regal jacket, and the outfit resembles ministerial garb. She is wearing an elaborate necklace, and around her head she has a glittery black headdress similar to the ones Ma Rainey often wore. Although the other divas join in this final number, Aretha is the featured performer, and as she works her way to the chorus, she contorts her face and stiffens her body in a vivid overture to both the sensual and the divine. For portions of the chorus she raises her hand in the air, gospel style, as if she is witnessing about God's mercy while she sings about the glory of sexual ecstasy when the right man comes along. This entanglement of sexuality and divinity is quite aptly captured in one line of the song during which Aretha declares that her new found man rescued her soul (*Divas Live*). The concert ends with Aretha leading the divas in an unexpected, overtly religious finale that consists of them all repeating "Jesus" in a variety of tonal inflections. This inarticulate repetition is actually quite appropriate as it suggests both the breathless and speechless aftermath of sexual intercourse as well as the incomprehensibility associated with the transformation that results from a divine religious experience.

In her study *The Holy Profane*, Teresa Reed explores the relationship between black religious and black secular music, and her conclusions help explain why Aretha so effortlessly flowed between two songs that on the surface appear quite disparate.[71] Reed proposes that these religious and secular musical traditions often merge boundaries because of their African roots: "In the West-African worldview, music is intrinsically spiritual, the sacred is intrinsically musical, and both music and the divine permeate every imaginable part of life" (5). She further elaborates by referring to renowned African American musician Thomas Dorsey:

> Dorsey himself considered the connection between gospel and blues to be self-evident, as the two styles had a similar emotional effect upon its participants. To [Dorsey], both were equally valid vehicles of feeling, and the nature of the feeling—sacred or secular—was unimportant. (11)

Dorsey's perspective helps illuminate Aretha's performance and recognizes the intimate nexus between the emotions aroused by a savior and those aroused by a lover—both sets of feelings related to a sort of metamorphosis.

Like Aretha, rapper Missy Elliott embraces this transformation trope as a critical element of her musical persona, and she has become incredibly successful at her art. After releasing a mass of chart-topping songs; earning scores of music awards, including two Grammies; and selling millions of albums, Missy (Melissa Elliott) is now rap music's premiere diva. She emerged onto the popular music landscape in 1997 with her debut album, *Supa Dupa Fly*; however, at that time Missy was already an established songwriter and producer, and she has worked with such big names as Christina Aguilera, Justin Timberlake and Beyonce Knowles.[72] Missy's talents extend beyond the performance arena, and she has put her entrepreneurial skill to the test as CEO of GoldMind Inc., her record label.[73] Unlike many other rappers, Missy writes and produces all of her songs—a daunting task for someone who has released six albums in seven years—and this level of involvement in her career has given her even greater agency in the spectacular nature of her performances.[74] Furthermore, she claims responsibility for ninety-seven percent of the content in her musical videos and accredits only the remaining three percent to the director.[75]

The hallmark characteristic of the images that Missy stages for herself, in both her musical videos and on her album covers, is best encapsulated by the notion of metamorphosis. In fact, the title of her 2002 album, *Under Construction*, could quite effectively function as the thematic mantra for Missy's look and many of her songs.[76] For example, the video of her hit "Get Ur Freak On" is built upon representations of transformation.[77] Several scenes from the video are set in the ruins of a building populated with ghoulish bodies, some hanging from the ceiling like germinating cocoons. As Missy sings the title of the song, some of these dormant bodies begin wriggling as they come to life, and this suggests that she merges the freakishness of hypersexuality—getting your freak on—with the freakishness of transformation and identity slippage.[78] In yet another scene she wears army fatigues and swings across the set from an elaborate chandelier, again repeating the title of the song, "Get Ur Freak On," which is directed at both her audience and a group of dancers below her. She is somber and almost militant as she repeats this phrase, and this implies that freakishness has been infused with a virulent militancy and is a requirement for survival. The dancers are wearing white body suits, accessorized with a nominal amount of camouflage gear, and their sensual dance routine is an obvious metaphor for sexual intercourse. Additionally, their white outfits suggest that these dancers are the ashen zombies who have come to life by complying with Missy's orders, again a merger of transformative capacity and sexuality.

In contrast to "Get Ur Freak On," which has strong sexual overtones, the images in most of Missy's videos are relatively asexual. In fact, she often stages herself in masculinized postures in terms of the way she asserts her gender position in relation to her dancers. Just as male rappers are often flanked by female dancers whose skimpy clothing and suggestive gyrations situate the women as cogent markers of hypersexuality, Missy often situates herself in her videos based on this paradigm, placing herself in the position of the male rapper. In fact, when Missy lost weight and the video for her hit "Work It" was released, Missy did not show off her new, lithe body.[79] Instead, she appears in baggy sweats with a bevy of female dancers who seem to be exposing their bodies on Missy's behalf. Even when Missy does reveal her new slender body on the cover of *This Is Not a Test*, she revisits her usual masculine paradigms. For the album cover she is dressed in a form-fitting trench coat that reveals her new figure, but this coat supports the staging of a highly militaristic scene involving an armed vehicle, a brooding pair of dogs, and other bodies dressed in military paraphernalia—the entire scene very evocative of Hitler's SS forces.

Despite Missy's inclination to often present herself as somewhat defeminized, almost always wearing male-styled pants and loosely fitted baggy clothing which do not reveal her feminine curves, her face is usually quite clearly feminized—her hair meticulously coiffed and makeup flawlessly applied to Missy's pretty face. By subverting strict rules of gender imaging, this cross-gendered representation aids in generating astonishment. Furthermore, Missy's penchant for metamorphosis registers her perception that the ability to defy culturally delineated identity niches is an act of subversion.

Missy's costume choices also reflect her embrace of an identity-defiant motif in her work. For example, her camouflage gear from the "Get Ur Freak On" video implies Missy's desire and capacity to conceal her identity. Another of her outfits in the video is a white jumpsuit that looks quite Elvisesque, complete with shiny studs. This jumpsuit suggests that Missy like Elvis recognizes the performative potential of minstrelsy—the assumption of an alternate persona. Elvis further informs Missy's persona because despite his death, his identity continues to remain volatile given regular Elvis sightings, which symbolically suggest he is still alive. Additionally, a plethora of Elvis impersonators propagate his identity in a variety of textures. Elvis' minstrelsy was multi-layered, first by his assumption of a black performance posture and then by his alleged post-mortem assumption of various other identities. While Missy does not permanently assume any alternate racial posture, both she and Elvis thrive on a perpetual identity slippage: Elvis before and after his death and Missy during her career.

Missy's lyrics for "Get Ur Freak On" further suggest the importance of the spectacle of her transformative capacity and her resistance to a stable identity as she sings, while in her army fatigues, that no one should try to replicate her identity (*Missy "Misdemeanor" Elliott: Hits of Miss E . . . The Videos*). She also addresses her audience's infatuation with her musical talents and recognizes the importance of her ability to create spectacle through metamorphosis when in her lyrics she acknowledges that her audience is impressed by her ability to "switch" her appearance (*Missy "Misdemeanor" Elliott: Hits of Miss E . . . The Videos*).

Missy plays with cultural identity and creates racially disruptive images of herself, contextualized by the notion of otherness. In videos like "She's a Bitch," Missy makes a spectacle of her fat black body by exaggerating its presumed foreignness, hence increasing its value as spectacular.[80] This move is similar to the "blacking up" that vaudevillians were required to undergo as a means of making their bodies an exaggeration of the excessive. In fact, Missy literally blackens herself for this video, which is set against a somewhat futuristic landscape. One of the opening images of Missy features her in a black jumpsuit that resembles a cross between a life jacket and a space suit. Her skin is blackened, seeming to almost merge into her clothing, and her head is bald. She is wearing something like goggles, and these are fitted over each eye in a very accurate representation of the facial features in some of the most widely circulated images of aliens. Additionally, small diamond studs are arranged on her scalp and the design creates the illusion of a cross between a Mohawk haircut and African tribal scars. In the Unites States, where whiteness is constructed as normative, Missy's costume astonishes by subverting presumptions of ethnic fixity and superimposing on her already deviant fat body evocations of Africans, Native Americans and alien beings.

Missy's combining of transformation and hypersexuality reveals her recognition that the stage welcomes her for her ability to astonish. She further realizes that resisting a fixed identity is a dangerous violation of the United States' cultural norms and that the society becomes quite anxious over ambivalent racial or gender identities, which increases the opportunities for such identity mergers to astonish. In the video for "She's a Bitch," Missy further engages the issue of identity slippage in a scene where she appears against a backdrop suggestive of a computer's interior.[81] Flashing neon lights approximate electrical wires and other computer hardware, and this decorative theme is carried over onto Missy's costume—a jumpsuit with neon streaks—so she appears to be almost subsumed within the belly of the computer's machinery and indistinguishable from the machine's components. This portion of the video underscores Missy's privileging of a transformation motif in her work and implies the agency of otherness in the functioning of America's social machinery. Although Missy appears to be engulfed in the system, she is in fact a separate entity contributing to the whole.

The lyrics for "She's a Bitch" further emphasize the song's transgressive undertones and add a verbal superimposition of unruliness on Missy's already disruptive and highly camouflaged body. Throughout the song Missy repeats the title "She's a Bitch," as a verbal resonator of the behavior she describes in the rest of the lyrics as well as a linguistic speculum of the video's storyline.[82] The protagonist "bitch" of the song is busy giving black eyes and busting lips while concurrently claiming her performative dominance when she sings of her musical prowess (*Missy "Misdemeanor" Elliott: Hits of Miss E . . . The Videos*). Furthermore, she invokes sexuality through the metaphor of fire, intertwining the performative space and female sexuality as sites of unruliness (*Missy "Misdemeanor" Elliott: Hits of Miss E . . . The Videos*).

Like Missy, rap music unabashedly embraces transgression as its hallmark characteristic—lewd lyrics, gaudy clothing, and militant themes all mark this genre as defiantly counter-culture. Missy Elliott's artistic exploitation of rap has mined this musical style for even more expressions of its transgressive qualities, and she has emerged as a twenty-first century chameleon of musical performance—a pop icon of transformation. She challenges American anxieties over unstable identities and stages herself in racially and sexually ambiguous postures. Rumors about Missy's own sexuality that suggest she is either gay or bisexual further support the transgressive image she has contrived for herself and that has contributed to her phenomenal success. Her songs and musical videos tease the notion of the spectacular, taking the already transgressive image of a fat black woman and propagating it in a variety of forms—making a spectacle of the creation of the spectacular.

Caribbean performative musical spaces are also venues for the staging of the spectacular, specifically within the framework of dancehall and calypso. Both musical genres are historically associated with disruption and colonial resistance and both present a perpetual challenge to neocolonial cultural norms. Dancehall, one of reggae's offshoots, originated in Kingston's inner-city ghettos, and the music disrupts Jamaica's Eurocentric codes of propriety on multiple planes. Sound system "clashes" are a regular and important feature of dancehall music and perhaps these events best help shape the most appropriate metaphor for defining the relationship between dancehall and the majority black Jamaican public. During a clash, groups of deejays affiliated with different sound systems try to outplay each other by selecting songs that best arouse the audience; additionally, the respective deejays compete based on their oratory skills. The conflictive context for these clashes mirrors dancehall's numerous other sites of contestation. For example, the promoters of outdoor street dances and neighbors in surrounding vicinities often clash over the noise from the sound system and issues of public disturbance. Additionally, the evolution of a "vulgar" dancehall cultural aesthetic, as well as its subversive lyrical content consisting of lewd sexual references, clashes with middle-class bourgeoisie propriety.[83] Furthermore, dancehall lyrics are rendered exclusively in the island's local dialect or *patois,* contesting the privileged position of English as Jamaica's authentic discourse.

Trinidadian calypso has a similar legacy of contestation. In the early twentieth century the term calypso came into use in association with Trinidadian carnival music.[84] One of carnival's earliest expressions was the weekend slave dance, which often came under the suspicion of the ruling planter classes as a venue for coordinating rebellion.[85] Calypso's intimate association with carnival helped fuel its rebellious posture, and this musical tradition started to attract many of the same criticisms currently associated with dancehall. According to calypso scholar Gordon Rohlehr, articles in the *Port of Spain Gazette* from around this period "usually complained about the obscene and abusive songs, as well as the disrespect shown by lower-class masqueraders to the high and mighty in the society" (47).

These complaints regarding calypso often found themselves specifically located on the site of the female body, and an 1884 article in the *Port of Spain Gazette* situates the young women of Trinidad as the locus for the country's moral decay:

> In Port of Spain we have shown how the bands had been cowed down, but the obscenities, the bawdy language and gestures of the women in the street have been pushed to a degree of wantonness which cannot be surpassed, and which must not be tolerated. Obscenities are no longer veiled under the cloak of words of doubtful meaning, but lechery, in all its naked brutality was sung, spoken and represented by disgusting gestures in our public streets. The growing generation of young girls will become the curse of the country if these yearly saturnalia are allowed to continue. (Rohlehr 31)

The "jamettes" to whom the article refers were women associated with both carnival and calypso, and their astonishing gyrations simultaneously attracted the public's attention and its disgruntlement. Within a pan-Caribbean context, these jamettes are the performative ancestors of the Jamaican dancehall queens as are Jamaican set girls. During slavery as a part of the Christmas season Jonkonnu festivities, set girls paraded through the streets of Jamaica festooned in elaborate clothing and competed with each other to see who was the best dressed.[86] These set girls as well as the jamettes have bequeathed their legacy of spectacular behavior that specifically manifests as dancehall's outrageous fashion.

Dancehall "divas" populate the literal dancehall, and their bodies are reflective sites for an emergent dancehall aesthetic.[87] Their notoriety within the dancehall setting expresses itself primarily on two planes: first with regard to their sexually explicit dance performances and second in terms of their elaborate fashion and accessories, which have perhaps become the most familiar visual expression of dancehall. However, unlike carnival, the dancehall operates in a contained space, and the public is not readily privy to the performances that take place within. As a result, the dancehall diva's ghetto fabulous style, which is readily observable on the streets of Jamaica, has become one of the primary targets of middle and upper-class disdain (along with dancehall lyrics disseminated on the radio stations). Just as over a century ago the jamette's "disgusting gestures" were situated as a source of national decline, so is the female dancehall body situated as a representation of cultural degradation.[88] In a 1994 newspaper article, Jamaican columnist Morris Cargill comments on the flesh-exposing *haute couture*, no doubt dancehall inspired, that had by then taken hold on the local fashion scene: "Males can become bored by over-exposure. Women's clothing, including bathing suits and including the crotch-cutters worn by beauty contestants, should titillate and promise, not hand out the prizes before they are won" (Cargill 217).

The tight and revealing nature of female dancehall fashion has not only led to national outrage but to attempts to police the Jamaican female body. In 1993 signs appeared at the Bustamante Children's Hospital in Kingston stipulating that dancehall fashion was not permitted in the waiting area of the emergency room.[89] Additionally, in preparation for the funeral of past Jamaican Prime Minister Michael Manley, guidelines were issued in the newspaper encouraging women to dress "appropriately."[90] This "encouragement" was particularly meaningful against the backdrop of another funeral gathering, that of Jim Brown, a popular don in the Kingston area.[91] One newspaper's fashion commentator conveyed her distaste for the mourners' apparel when she stated that "No mini was too short, no tights too tight, no chiffon too sheer, no lace too see through"; moreover, she summed up the women's dress as a "homage to bareness" (Soas, qtd. in Ulysse 164).

Both dancehall and calypso are musical traditions associated with acts that generate astonishment. Aside from their politically and sexually charged lyrics, both traditions are contextualized within the unruly dance/performance rituals of carnival and dancehall, which feature the extensive costuming of the female body in highly revealing attire. The fat black woman's body has come to play an instrumental role in the creation of spectacle in these two performative spaces, keeping in mind that dancehall's performative territory extends beyond the physical location of the hall to the fashion performance of dancehall all around Jamaica. Fat bodies contribute to the disruptive spectacle of these two expressive forms, primarily because of the hypersexualizing of those bodies, which is immediately apparent in dancehall tradition. Dancehall has been the venue for the exposure of the fat black female body beyond the platform of the hefty higgler whose association with food and later the supply of scarce imported goods helped to firmly cross-pollinate her social function as both a literal supplier of goods and an icon of abundance. Gina Ulysse suggests that "Dancehall not only projected this full black female form into public arenas, but asserted both its desirability and sexuality" (159).

Nowhere has this projection of the large sexualized black body been more apparent than with the unofficial crowning and sustained reign of Carlene the dancehall queen. Carlene came to power in the dancehall arena in the early 1990s via a series of fashion clashes in which she and her posse of women competed against professional models from a local agency.[92] Carlene and her crew were situated as a part of the underprivileged Jamaican masses, although technically they did not necessarily fit into this category, while the bodies of the professional models were read as middle/upper-class commodities. The models performed fashion appropriations of female behavior that fell within the boundaries of middle-class propriety, but Carlene and her group set out to astonish. Uninhibited by codes of female propriety, at one clash, barely clad in fishnet and lingerie, Carlene did a dance routine in which she imitated the experience of an orgasm.[93] This willingness to shock her audiences by engaging in sexually risqué behavior has helped Carlene become a permanent fixture in Jamaican popular culture, and she has appeared on television for a variety of commercials, has been spokesperson for a brand of condoms, and now hosts a talk show.

However, Carlene's ascendancy to fame is complicated because not only is she full-figured, she is also mixed-race and very light-skinned. Carlene's embrace by Jamaica's corporate world suggests that her "brownness" has facilitated her corporate and social mobility by rendering her crude public displays more palatable since the site of enactment is a brown and not black body.[94] Nevertheless, Carlene's size has been instrumental in her success and in sustaining her popularity with the black working class on whose approval she is ultimately dependent. Her fat is an evocation of blackness that helps to resituate her near-white body as a part of the extended body politic of Jamaica's masses.

In Trinidad, size has an equally compelling role in carnival/calypso iconography, and a number of female calypsonians are women of size. Calypso Rose, Singing Sandra, and Lady Iere are among several fat black women whose bodies reflect the subversive lyrics of their music and the disruptive potential of calypso in general. Soca has become to calypso what dancehall is to reggae, its most recent offshoot, and one of the very popular contemporary soca artists is Denise Belfon, a fat black woman famed for her energetic performances. According to Denise, "People are always amazed at how a woman my size could move so I think a lot of women respect me for that" ("Denise Belfon").[95] This comment indicates how Denise's size contributes to the spectacular nature of her performances because audiences are amused by the assumingly incongruous juxtaposition of her large body and her energetic dancing capabilities. Because of Denise's singing and performance skills she has received numerous recognitions in the soca arena. In 1995 *Everybody's Magazine* in New York gave her the award for Emerging Artist.[96] The Ragga Soca Awards have nominated her in the Best Female Soca Artist category on several occasions, and in 1998 and 1999 she won the title.[97] Interestingly, Denise names Aretha Franklin, Billie Holiday and Mahalia Jackson as important artistic influences—all women whose full bodies helped create the spectacle of their performance and aided in their success.

While both Jamaica and Trinidad do not have a dominant white majority, the gender and racial issues identified with regard to performative spaces in the United States are still relevant in the Caribbean's cultural environment. This similarity occurs because the same Eurocentric cultural ideology that informs American beliefs, an ideology that arises from the New World's shared colonial legacy, operates in the Caribbean in a transmuted state in the form of bourgeoisie and middle-class cultural values. These values are often underscored with strains of quasi-religious propriety and traverse color boundaries in their manifestation. This slippage from the more distinct racial/ideological boundaries identified in the United States occurs because the Caribbean's vision of race has a greater degree of class inflection than it does in the United States. Hence, behavioral choices within a Caribbean context can with greater ease than in the United States either "blacken" or "whiten" a person's identity. So while the soca and dancehall performative spaces are not exclusively black, these arenas are quite distinctly associated with the black, working-class majority, and any behavioral habits associated with these spaces carry undercurrents of blackness.

With these class issues in mind, Carlene's and Denise's large bodies may also be read within the context of the carnivalesque. In Mikhail Bakhtin's text *Rabelais and His World,* he describes the carnivalesque as a mode of resistance to high-brow culture, and this resistance is accomplished via a redeployment of "proper" upper-class rituals such as language and fashion.[98] The carnivalesque aspects of carnival and dancehall activities—the elaborate hair, makeup and costumes—comprise a sort of role-playing, a pretence at being part of the upper class. The fat black woman neatly fits into this inverted order because she is not beautiful according to Eurocentric aesthetics just as the carnival/dancehall participants are not wealthy. This is why her body is such a dominant image in these performative spaces; it encapsulates the inverted essence of the space.

The beginning of this chapter questioned why fat white women were not embraced in North American performative spaces the way that Carlene, Denise, or Missy have been in their respective cultures. It is because fat white women personify conflicted representations. Their whiteness marks them as an ideal embodiment of womanhood while their fatness evokes the unruliness and disobedience associated with black skin. Consequently, several of the large white women who have succeeded in the American entertainment industry have done so by erasing all signs of unruliness, such as singer and actress Kate Smith, whose rendition of "God Bless America" firmly anchored her as a symbol of American patriotism and resituated her fat as a maternal signifier.[99] Similarly, Carnie Wilson of the Wilson Phillips trio used her pretty face and sweet smile to evoke innocence. Interestingly, since losing over 150 pounds, she has accepted a proposal to pose for a nude spread, an act that would certainly have raised virulent opposition had it taken place while she was fat.[100] On the other hand, women like Roseanne Barr and Anna Nicole Smith have forgone any conformist efforts and instead capitalize on the already unruly essence of their large bodies.

The blues, rhythm and blues, soca and dancehall are all musical traditions that operate with a similarly unruly essence in the realm of the carnivalesque. These genres have emerged from a social legacy of racism and oppression, and the rituals associated with each style of music address that oppressive heritage. Fat black women have contributed to the musical engagement of this shared diasporic experience of marginalization by providing bodily sites which counter the aesthetic values of the historically white hegemony. Additionally, these bodies gain popularity because in the African Diaspora they are more readily seen as an acceptable, and in some cases more desirable, form of embodiment. Furthermore, largeness has come to symbolize abundance and prosperity, especially important signifiers throughout the African Diaspora, which has undergone perpetual economic marginalization. The specifics of how large female bodies debase propriety varies across the disaporic genres, but the hypersexual connotations attendant on these large bodies seem to specifically inform the quality of their disruptive nature.

NOTES

1. Kris Green, "Waterman to Quit 'Pop Idol,'" *Digital Spy* (March 16, 2004), accessed June 26, 2004, <www.digitalspy.co.uk/article/ds13913.html>.
2. Green, "Waterman to Quit 'Pop Idol.'"
3. Ed Boyle, "British Pounds-a-Plenty," *CBSnews.com*, March 26, 2004, CBS News, accessed May 6, 2004, <http://cbsnews.com/stories/2004/03/26/uttm/main608783.shtml>.

4. Allison Samuels, "Wall of Soul: Jill Scott Is Part of a Generation of 'Neo-Soul' Artists Who Are Reinventing a Classic Tradition while still 'Keeping It Real' for Black Audiences," *Newsweek* (April 9, 2000), Expanded Academic ASAP, Infotrac, University of Miami, accessed April 8, 2004, <http://web3.infotrac.galegroup.com>.

5. Donald Bogle, *Brown Sugar* (New York: Harmony Books, 1980), 31.

6. Lorraine Ali, "Princess of Soul: Until She Wears Aretha's Crown, Angie Stone Is Happy Just To Sing," *Newsweek* (November 12, 2001), Expanded Academic ASAP, Infotrac, University of Miami, accessed April 8, 2004, <http://web3.infotrac.galegroup.com>; Angie Stone, *Black Diamond*. Arista, 1999.

7. "The Fifty Most Beautiful People in the World 2001—Jill Scott," *People Weekly* 55, no. 19 (May 14, 2000): 148, Expanded Academic ASAP, Infotrac, University of Miami, accessed April 8, 2004, <http://web3.infotrac.galegroup.com>.

8. Melody K. Hoffman, "Hip-hop Innovator Missy Elliott: Reinvents Herself-Again-With New CD 'This Is Not a Test!'" *Jet* 105, no. 2 (Jan. 12, 2004): 58, Expanded Academic ASAP, Infotrac, University of Miami, accessed April 8, 2004, <http://web3.infotrac.galegroup.com>.

9. Hoffman, "Hip-hop Innovator Missy Elliott."

10. Lynn Norment, "Queen Latifah's Roller-coaster Ride to the Top," *Ebony* 58, no. 6 (April 2003): 152, Expanded Academic ASAP, Infotrac, University of Miami, accessed April 8, 2004, <http://web3.infotrac.galegroup.com>.

11. "Queen Latifah," *The Internet Movie Database*, accessed April 8, 2004, <www.imdb.com/name/nm0001451/>.

12. "The Fifty Most Beautiful People in the World 2003—Queen Latifah," *People Weekly* 59, no. 18 (May 12, 2003): 110, Expanded Academic ASAP, Infotrac, University of Miami, accessed April 8, 2004, <http://web3.infotrac.galegroup.com>; "The Fifty Most Beautiful People in the World 2001—Jill Scott."

13. From as early as 1994, white consumers purchased 75 percent of hard-core rap albums. Marc Spiegler, "Marketing Street Culture: Bringing Hip-Hop Style to the Mainstream," *American Demographics* 18, no. 11 (Nov. 1996): 28–35, Expanded Academic ASAP, Infotrac, University of Miami, accessed August 9, 2004, <http://web3.infotrac.galegroup.com>.

14. Spiegler, "Marketing Street Culture."

15. I would also add that the extensive use of hip-hop culture as a marketing tool capitalizes upon the genre's potential as a transformative site for escape and rebellion.

16. The *American Idol* series is a talent competition that airs in the United States on the Fox network.

17. Thomas Riis, "Blacks on the Musical Stage," *Images of Blacks in American Culture*, ed. Jessie Carney Smith (New York: Greenwood Press, 1988), 31.

18. Riis, "Blacks on the Musical Stage," 31.

19. Riis, "Blacks on the Musical Stage," 31.

20. Robert C. Toll, *Blacking Up: The Minstrel Show in Nineteenth-Century America* (New York: Oxford University Press, 1974), 33.

21. Susan A. Glenn, *Female Spectacle: The Theatrical Roots of Modern Feminism* (Cambridge, Mass.: Harvard University Press, 2000), 2.

22. Glenn, *Female Spectacle*, 40–41.

23. Glenn, *Female Spectacle*, 56.
24. Glenn, *Female Spectacle*, 56.
25. Glenn, *Female Spectacle*, 56–57.
26. Glenn, *Female Spectacle*, 57.
27. Glenn, *Female Spectacle*, 60.
28. Glenn, *Female Spectacle*, 60.
29. Glenn, *Female Spectacle*, 61.
30. Sophie Tucker, *Some of These Days: The Autobiography of Sophie Tucker* (Garden City, N.Y.: Doubleday, Doran & Company, Inc., 1945).
31. Tucker, *Some of These Days*, 35.
32. Glenn, *Female Spectacle*, 50.
33. Glenn, *Female Spectacle*, 52.
34. Glenn suggests that turn-of-the-century "female performers became agents and metaphors of changing gender relations" and that the theater was a space for "acting out and staging the cultural, social, and political assertions as well as the anxieties associated with" this period (3).
35. Michael D. Basil, "Identification as a Mediator of Celebrity Effects," *Journal of Broadcasting & Electronic Media* 40 (Fall 1996): 478–95. See Basil's discussion of celebrity identification in which he suggests that the effectiveness of a celebrity endorser is dependent on an audience's ability to identify with that celebrity.
36. J. D. Williams and W. J. Qualls, "Middle-class Black Consumers and the Intensity of Ethnic Identification," *Psychology and Marketing* 6 (1989): 263–86.
37. Sander M. Abend and Michael S. Porter, "Identification," *Psychoanalysis: The Major Concepts*, eds. Burness Moore and Bernard D. Fine (New Haven, Conn.: Yale University Press, 1995), 463; Sigmund Freud, *The Interpretation of Dreams*, trans. James Strachey (New York: Avon Books, 1965).
38. Glenn, *Female Spectacle*, 61.
39. See my discussion of hypersexuality in chapter two.
40. While the focus of this project is on musical performers, there are large black women working in the entertainment industry in a variety of capacities and their careers are also informed by the conditions. I suggest, for example, Oprah and Star Jones.
41. Robert Santelli, "A Century of the Blues," *Martin Scorsese Presents The Blues: A Musical Journey*, eds. Peter Guralnick et al. (New York: Amistad, 2003), 14.
42. Santelli, "A Century of the Blues," 14.
43. In fact, the signification of these women's bodies as tropes for abundance situates their performance more definitively in the world of the carnivalesque, for if wealth and abundance were the domain of the white majority, then Bessie Smith or Ida Cox's fat body suggests that their performances effect a form of white role playing—a reversal of traditional minstrelsy.
44. See Handy's autobiography: W. C. Handy, *Father of the Blues: An Autobiography by W. C. Handy* (London: Sidgwick & Jackson, 1957).
45. Daphne Duval Harrison, *Black Pearls: Blues Queens of the 1920s* (New Brunswick, N.J.: Rutgers University Press, 1988), 35. See Harrison for more details on Ma Rainey's recording history; Bogle, *Brown Sugar*, 21. Also see Bogle for information on Ma Rainey's career.
46. Bogle, *Brown Sugar*, 21.

47. Bogle, *Brown Sugar*, 18.
48. Sandra R. Lieb, *Mother of the Blues: A Study of Ma Rainey* (Amherst: University of Massachusetts Press, 1981), 8.
49. Lieb, *Mother of the Blues*, 10.
50. Lieb, *Mother of the Blues*, 11.
51. Bob Hayes, "Ma Rainey's Review," *Chicago Defender*, February 13, 1926.
52. Lieb, *Mother of the Blues*, xiv.
53. Lieb, *Mother of the Blues*, xiv.
54. Lieb, *Mother of the Blues*, 82.
55. Lieb, *Mother of the Blues*, 82.
56. Lieb, *Mother of the Blues*, 110.
57. Lieb, *Mother of the Blues*, 18.
58. Lieb, *Mother of the Blues*, 17.
59. Lieb, *Mother of the Blues*, 17.
60. Lieb, *Mother of the Blues*, 18.
61. Bogle, *Brown Sugar*, 16. Ma Rainey was rumored to be bisexual, further enhancing the transgressive quality of her persona.
62. Bogle, *Brown Sugar*, 18.
63. Aretha Franklin, "Respect," *Respect*, Wea, 2002; Aretha Franklin, "(You Make me Feel Like a) Natural Woman," *Respect*, Wea, 2002; Aretha Franklin, "I Never Loved a Man (The Way I Love You)," *Respect*, Wea, 2002.
64. Stephen Holden, "Playful Aretha Franklin Plumbs Roots of Soul," *New York Times*, Nov. 5, 1994, late ed.: 15.
65. Aretha Franklin and David Ritz, *Aretha: From These Roots* (New York: Villard Books, 1999).
66. bell hooks, *Black Looks: Race and Representation* (Boston: South End Press, 1992).
67. "The Original Do-Right Woman: The Queen of Soul Talks about Her Life, Her Loves, Her Fear of Flying and the Time She and Sam Cooke 'Almost Went There,'" *Newsweek* 134, no. 14 (Oct. 4, 1999): 68.
68. *Divas Live*, directed by Michael A. Simon, starring Mariah Carey, Gloria Estefan, Shania Twain, Aretha Franklin, Celine Dion, and Carole King, Epic Music Video, 1998.
69. *Divas Live*.
70. Sarandon specifically refers to Aretha's demands for "respect" in the 1960s as a universal call on everyone's behalf; however, Sarandon's comment strikes me as a subconscious effort by the white/male power structure to dilute the black and female undertones of the song. This act of ostensibly embracing Aretha seems more an act of delivering her artistry from its racialized and gendered roots, hence making her otherness less specific to certain socio-historical occurrences.
71. Teresa Reed, *The Holy Profane* (Lexington: University Press of Kentucky, 2003).
72. Lorraine Ali and Jennifer Ordonez, "The Marketing of Missy: The Electrifying Ms. Elliott Gets Commodified," *Newsweek* (Dec. 8, 2003): 100, Expanded Academic ASAP, Infotrac, University of Miami, accessed April 8, 2004, <http://web3.infotrac.galegroup.com>; Missy Elliott, *Supa Dupa Fly*, Elektra, 1997.

73. Hoffman, "Hip-hop Innovator Missy Elliott."
74. Ali and Ordonez, "The Marketing of Missy."
75. *Missy "Misdemeanor" Elliott: Hits of Miss E . . . The Videos*, starring Missy Elliott, Elektra, 2001.
76. Missy Elliott, *Under Construction*, Elektra, 2002.
77. *Missy "Misdemeanor" Elliott: Hits of Miss E . . . The Videos.*
78. Patricia Hill Collins, *Black Sexual Politics: African Americans, Gender, and the New Racism* (New York: Routledge, 2004), 127. Collins suggests that among black women performers sexuality has to function in numerous capacities because it is one of the few promotional tools available to them.
79. "Work It," VH1, March 17, 2003.
80. *Missy "Misdemeanor" Elliott: Hits of Miss E . . . The Videos.*
81. *Missy "Misdemeanor" Elliott: Hits of Miss E . . . The Videos.*
82. The term "bitch" also speaks to the notion of transformative capacity since the process of becoming a bitch suggests the movement from human to animal. See Patricia Hill Collins who suggests that the term bitch is often used in a contestational manner as opposed to its traditional derogatory usage (120).
83. Carolyn Cooper, *Noises in the Blood: Orality, Gender, and the "Vulgar" Body of Jamaican Popular Culture* (Durham, N.C.: Duke University Press, 1995). I use the term "vulgar" in keeping with Cooper's use of the term.
84. Errol Hill, "On the Origin of the Term, Calypso," *Ethnomusicology* 11, no. 3 (1967): 359–67. Hill suggests that the initial use of the term "calypso" in reference to Trinidadian carnival songs was in the *Port of Spain Gazette* in 1900.
85. Gordon Rohlehr, *Calypso and Society in Pre-independence Trinidad* (Port of Spain: Gordon Rohlehr, 1990), 3.
86. Avia Ustanny, "200 Years of Christmas," *Jamaica Gleaner Online* (Dec. 15, 2001), accessed Nov. 29, 2005, <www.jamaica-gleaner.com/gleaner/20011215/life/life2.html>.
87. Norman C. Stolzoff, *Wake the Town and Tell the People: Dancehall Culture in Jamaica* (Durham, N.C.: Duke University Press, 2000), xiii. I am indebted to Stolzoff for the term "dancehall diva."
88. Belinda Edmondson, "Public Spectacles: Caribbean Women and the Politics of Public Performance," *Small Axe* 7, no. 1 (2003): 1–16. See Edmondson's essay for a discussion of how female public performance in the Caribbean has been invested with nationalistic representational value.
89. Gina Ulysse, "Uptown Ladies and Downtown Women: Female Representations of Class and Color in Jamaica," *Ariel* (1999), 165.
90. Ulysse, "Uptown Ladies and Downtown Women," 164–65.
91. A "don" refers to inner city area leaders who often control their territory through a combination of illegal activities, including drug trafficking and blackmail.
92. Ulysse, "Uptown Ladies and Downtown Women," 161.
93. Ulysse, "Uptown Ladies and Downtown Women," 162.
94. Edmondson, "Public Spectacles," 7.
95. "Denise Belfon: Saucy Babe," Queenofsoca.com, accessed June 14, 2004, <http://queenofsoca.com/ProfileDenise.html>.
96. "Denise Belfon: Saucy Babe."

97. "Denise Belfon: Saucy Babe."

98. Mikhail Bakhtin, *Rabelais and His World*, trans. Helene Iswolsky (Cambridge, Mass.: MIT Press, 1968).

99. "Kate Smith Biography," accessed May 6, 2004, <http://katesmith.org/katebio.html>.

100. Deborah Roberts, "A Whole New Her: After Dropping 150 Pounds, Carnie Wilson Is Taking on New Challenges," ABCNews, May 30, 2004, accessed June 30, 2004, <www.abcnews.go.com/sections/2020/Entertainment/Wilson030530_Carnie.html>.

Conclusion

Consumption and Control

The "Epidemic" of Fatness

In the contemporary Western world, slenderness has come to represent the equivalent of good health. This equating of slenderness with fitness and longevity is especially apparent in the United States, where fatness has been named an "obesity epidemic"—a title that pathologizes the fat body as an epicenter of disease and deterioration. Given that only a century ago Americans perceived fat, voluptuous bodies such as Lillian Russell's as both desirable and attractive, how is it that bodies sometimes bordering on a state of emaciation now dominate America's notion of aesthetic and physiological superiority? An interesting link exists between America's consumerist culture and its choice of bodily ideal, and the glorification of slenderness is both a subconscious effort to divert attention from America's greed as well as a capitalist mass-marketing strategy.

Shopping has become one of America's most beloved pastimes. No longer a need-based activity, shopping visits to the mall or Super Wal-Mart are leisurely family affairs. This act of shopping for pleasure has contributed to a surge in American debt, and in 2004 the national consumer debt figures reached an all time high of over two *trillion* dollars—double the one trillion figure reached in 1994.[1] A hallmark of America's current consumption rage has been the multiple-purchase phenomenon. It is now passé to own only one of just about anything, and most households seem to have several motor vehicles, television sets, computers, stereos and DVD players to name a few multiple-purchase items. Some new homes even have three and four garages, while others come fitted with double ovens plus a microwave. While America may epitomize consumerist gluttony, these purchasing patterns are evident throughout the Western world and in some parts of the developing world highly influenced by Western cultural values. These similarities in consumption patterns, encouraged through globalization and mass-marketing strategies, account for the West's shared aesthetic ideal, as well as the embrace of these values in other parts of the world.

It is in response to this unprecedented level of consumerism that requirements of slenderness have dominated Western aesthetics as a subconscious diversionary tactic that compensates for the culture's diminished financial health. By taking anxieties over the society's loss of control of its financial body and resituating these anxieties on the physical body, imperatives of slenderness falsely comfort by suggesting that control of body size registers control in other arenas.[2] Consequently, the anticipated results of fiscal prudence—happiness, economic longevity and financial health—have been positioned as the reward for astutely managing the human body to achieve a state that mirrors the leanness of financial constraints the culture desires but cannot accomplish.

In the Western world and in many postcolonial cultures, not only slenderness but whiteness is a highly privileged physical commodity, and this aesthetic marginalization of large black women intervenes upon their literary portrayal as well as the iconography of these women in the popular culture. This project addresses these concerns. While many scholars working in literary and cultural studies have written about the body, very few have addressed fatness as a central physiological feature, and even fewer have focused on representations of the fat black woman. This project begins to fill that vacuum with an interdisciplinary approach to assessing the textual and cultural significance of the fat black female body.

In the contemporary African Diaspora, the fat black woman's body occupies a largely resistive and transgressive space, despite the fact, and because of the fact that some of the earlier images and literary representations of that body, shaped mostly by white hegemonic culture, were part of an effort to diminish black womanhood. This historical devaluation was often constructed within the realm of sexuality and took the form of either desexualization, for example in the iconography of the Mammy in the United States and the higgler in the Caribbean, or on the other hand hypersexualization in the iconography and display of the Hottentot Venus.[3] In response to this devaluation, the neo-resistant spirit embedded in representations of the large black woman arises from an intended exaggeration of either of these hegemonically sponsored efforts to diminish black womanhood.

On one hand, representations of fat black women in literature and in popular culture establish her body as a poignant site of sexuality, its sensuousness unabashedly embellished beyond the hegemonically sponsored representation. A telling example is the highly sexualized performances of Carlene the dancehall queen from Jamaica.[4] Because Carlene's performance is self-authored, her feisty and "vulgar" recasting of the hypersexualized large black female body is in many ways a subconscious retaliation to the dehumanizing exhibit of the Hottentot Venus's caged body and more generally to the historical objectification of black female bodies throughout the African Diaspora. Furthermore, Carlene performs with the recognition that her gyrations and scantily clad body offend the religiously underscored Western behavioral norms of Jamaican society. Additionally, the women, both fat and slender, who attend the dancehall and expose their bodies within that performative arena and on the streets of Jamaica at large similarly engage in their fleshy displays as both a celebration of their sexuality as well as a subconscious class-inflected social affront. This retaliatory affront is propelled by both collective and individual subconscious responses to contemporary manifestations of economic as well as social marginalization, a marginalization that shares similar roots with the racialized oppression enacted against the Venus Hottentot.

Some may interpret Carlene's sexual agency as problematic, or for that matter the sexual agency exhibited by performers Ma Rainey and Missy Elliott, or literary characters Miss B in *The Duppy* and the full-bodied narrator of *The Fat Black Woman's Poems*. Because these women and literary characters alike engage their sexuality in a raw and explicit fashion, there may be difficulty reading this engagement as empowering because of the supposedly deviant nature of these women's behavior. However, this problem only arises if Carlene's dancing and Miss B's sexual enthusiasm are read within the framework of Western, Judeo-Christian behavioral norms and gendered sexual regulation. Beyond the constraints of these or any other behavioral codes, there is no stable reading of this "deviant" sexual agency; the choice to perform in these sexually unruly ways is iconoclastic and in turn a form of chosen sexual impropriety and resistance.

The other dominant neo-resistant representational mode with regard to the portrayal of fat black women is anchored in a sort of economic retaliation. This retaliation is in response to the docility and resignation inherent in the socioeconomic status with which images of the African American Mammy figure, and less so the historic figure of the Caribbean market woman, are invested. The result has been an embellishment of the African association between fatness, health and fertility (evident in the fatting house rituals) and the fat black woman's body has become the representational site for both material and spiritual abundance. Ma Kilman's healing skills in *Omeros*, and Morris Cargill's depiction of the aggressive higgler all situate the bodies of large black woman as an outer reflection of their spiritual or economic abundance. What is further noteworthy is how these images prevail throughout the Diaspora. The Mama Benz cloth traders of Togo, renowned for both their size and their wealth, preside over their stalls with a queenly aura and traverse the streets of Togo in Mercedes Benz motor vehicles after which they are named.[5] These women are lateral projections of the same characteristics from which Ma Kilman and the higgler have sprung.

Because this project is grounded in an acknowledgment of the cultural sub-architecture that connects the African Diaspora, its research will provide a model for scholars who wish to implement their critical speculations on a diasporic basis and to extend these speculations with diasporic underscoring. Additionally, it offers multiple frameworks for the reading of the large black female body, frameworks that extend pre-existent research on the body and that cover new theoretical territory.

There is more research to be done related to fatness and race. For example, large black women in the performative space engage in acts of transgression unrelated to sexual impropriety. Women like Jamaican folklorist, poet, actress and performance artist Louise Bennett, better known as Miss Lou; rappers Queen Latifah and Sister Souljah; and singer Miriam Makeba resist hegemonic marginalization by becoming political advocates of their respective cultures and by directly engaging social concerns via their performances. Of all private and public figures in Jamaica, Miss Lou has probably made the most outstanding efforts towards legitimizing her country's dialect, while both Queen Latifah and Miriam Makeba address pressing social and political concerns in their respective societies.[6] Even Queen Latifah's performance title of "queen" and the name of one of her albums, *All Hail the Queen*, seek to reclaim black womanhood by exalting it.[7]

Another potential research trajectory is masculine discourses surrounding the fat black woman's body, specifically those discourses in the form of poetry and song. Throughout the Diaspora a range of songs and poems focus upon the woman's body, and these discourses construct female fatness in unique ways. The fat black woman's body is frequently celebrated as an agent of desire. In the Caribbean, dancehall deejay Sean Paul sings of his sexy "punkie" with whom he is in love, while American rap artist Sir Mix-a-Lot invokes fatness as a component of sexuality when he defiantly states his love of fleshy butts.[8] He further asserts his position by devaluing the slender bodies of supermodels.[9]

An excellent example of similar discourse which indirectly celebrates female fatness is the poem *Song of Lawino and Song of Ocol* by Ugandan poet Okot p'Bitek; it is a lament by a woman (Lawino) whose husband (Ocol) has chosen to take another wife and no longer finds his first wife attractive (36). The poem situates the gaunt body of a husband's new wife as a site of cultural deterioration in relation to his first wife's more ample body, and p'Bitek further extends this metaphor of slenderness by directly equating it to whiteness (37).

In addition to male discourses such as p'Bitek's, another interesting arm of exploration for other scholars is the literary and cultural positioning of fat white women. Texts like Peggy Payne's *Sister India* and Margaret Atwood's *Lady Oracle* and films such as *What's Eating Gilbert Grape?* and *Shallow Hal* all offer new territory for scholars to expand their understanding of how race and body size intersect. Aditionally, I challenge scholars to explore representations of fat men and how the legacy of disproportionate attention to women's bodies impacts the representational politics for men of both races.

One thing this project has made clear is that the vagaries of modern beauty culture and the unrelenting insistence on slenderness as a physiological ideal share the superficial objective of rewarding those whose bodies qualify as beautiful. However, modern beauty culture's ultimate goal is not rewarding those bodies that comply with its stipulations of beauty, but punishing those that do not. While we can read beauty culture as a sort of genderized masochism, manifesting as four-inch stiletto heels, eating disorders, and bleached skin, it amounts to more. It is an effective way to corral women's pride and self-esteem but also an economical means of concomitantly punishing bodies that don't comply with whiteness. And so the rigors through which many fat black women must go to even approach the modern beauty boundaries are not so much a result of these bodies not being beautiful but ultimately punishment for their not being either white or male.

It is in reply to this assault that the fat black woman's body functions as a counteractive instrument that responds to the impact of (neo)colonization. She is a repository of latent energy and engages the Western idealization of whiteness and slenderness with her unruliness and rebellion, implicit in her size. Literary characters like Miss B in *The Duppy*, Mammy in *The Wind Done Gone*, the protagonist of *The Fat Black Woman's Poems* and Ma Kilman in *Omeros* use their disruptive and unruly behavior to exact control in the face of racial and gendered oppression. Similarly fat black women who are historical and popular culture icons such as the Caribbean higgler, Mary Seacole, Louise Bennett, Missy Elliott, and Mo'Nique of *The Parkers* are all invested with an aura of disobedience, anchored in their fatness and blackness. The hyper-embodiment of these fat black women (both literary and real) is also a symbolic form of resistance to their negation from Western history and culture, and the site of their fat black bodies affirm that whiteness and slenderness are not ideal states of embodiment.

NOTES

1. "U.S. Consumer Debt Growth 'Alarming,'" *United Press International*, Jan. 13, 2004, Expanded Academic ASAP, Infotrac, University of Miami, accessed July 17, 2004, <http: / / web3.infotrac.galegroup.com>.

2. Other fears over deteriorating control in areas such as time management contribute this displacement of anxieties to the realm of the physical body; however, financial concerns seems to underscore this transferal phenomenon.

3. *The Life and Times of Sara Baartman the Hottentot Venus*, directed by Zola Maseko, First Run/Icarus Films, 1998.

4. Gina Ulysse, "Uptown Ladies and Downtown Women: Female Representations of Class and Color in Jamaica," *Ariel* (1999): 162. See Ulysse for details on Carlene's rise to fame.

5. *Mama Benz: An African Market Woman*, directed by Katia Forbert Petersen, videocasette, SFINX Film/TV, 1993. See the documentary *Mama Benz* for more details on the life of these outstanding entrepreneurs.

6. *Visiting With Miss Lou*, videocassette, Creative Production and Training Center, 2003.

7. Queen Latifah, *All Hail the Queen*, Tommy Boy, 1989.

8. Sean Paul, "Punkie," *Dutty Rock*, Atlantic, 2003; Sir Mix-a-Lot, "Baby Got Back," *Mack Daddy*, American, 2002.

9. Sir Mix-a-Lot, "Baby Got Back."

Bibliography

Abend, Sander M., and Michael S. Porter. "Identification." P. 463 in *Psychoanalysis: The Major Concepts*, eds. Burness Moore and Bernard D. Fine. New Haven, Conn.: Yale University Press, 1995.

Abraham, Linus. "The Black Woman as Marker of Hypersexuality in Western Mythology: A Contemporary Manifestation in the Film *The Scarlet Letter*." *Journal of Communication Inquiry* 26, no. 2 (April 2002): 201.

Ali, Lorraine. "Princess of Soul: Until She Wears Aretha's Crown, Angie Stone Is Happy Just to Sing." *Newsweek* (Nov. 12, 2001). Expanded Academic ASAP. Infotrac. University of Miami. Accessed April 8, 2004, <http://web3.infotrac.galegroup.com>.

———, and Jennifer Ordonez. "The Marketing of Missy: The Electrifying Ms. Elliott Gets Commodified." *Newsweek* (Dec. 8, 2003): 100. Expanded Academic ASAP. Infotrac. University of Miami. Accessed April 8, 2004, <http://web3.infotrac.galegroup.com>.

Andrews, Larry. "Black Sisterhood in Gloria Naylor's Novels." *College Language Association Journal* 33, no. 1 (Sept. 1989): 1–25.

Angelou, Maya. "Phenomenal Woman." *The Complete Collected Poems of Maya Angelou*. New York: Random House, 1994.

Anthe, Marianne. "'Black Names' Get Snub in Job Study." *MSNBC*. BET.com. Accessed July 29, 2003, <http://stacks.msnbc.com/news/859373.asp?cp1=1#BODY>. Path: News; Race in America.

Aristotle. *Generation of Animals*. Trans. A. L. Peck. Cambridge, Mass.: Harvard University Press, 1953.

Aubry, Erin J. "The Butt: Its Politics, Its Profanity, Its Power." *Body Outlaws*. Ed. Ophira Edut. New York: Seal Press, 2000.

Bakhtin, Mikhail. *Rabelais and His World*. Trans. Helene Iswolsky. Cambridge, Mass.: MIT Press, 1968.

Bana, Hershini. "The Political Economy of Food." *Proteus* 17, no. 1 (Spring 2000): 18–24.

Banet-Weiser, Sarah. *The Most Beautiful Girl in the World*. Berkeley: University of California Press, 1999.

Barnes, Natasha. "Face of the Nation: Race, Nationalisms and Identities in Jamaican Beauty Pageants." *Massachusetts Review* 35, nos. 3–4 (Fall 1994): 471–92.

Bartky, Sandra Lee. "Foucault, Femininity, and the Modernization of Patriarchal Power." Pp. 129–54 in *Writing on the Body: Female Embodiment and Feminist Theory*, eds. Katie Conboy, Nadia Medina, and Sarah Stanbury. New York: Columbia University Press, 1997.

Basil, Michael D. "Identification as a Mediator of Celebrity Effects." *Journal of Broadcasting & Electronics Media* 40 (Fall 1996): 478–95.

Bass, Margaret K. "On Being a Fat Black Girl in a Fat-Hating Culture." Pp. 219–30 in *Recovering the Black Female Body: Self-Representations by African American Women*, eds. Michael Bennett and Vanessa D. Dickerson. New Brunswick, N.J.: Rutgers University Press, 2001.

Beckles, Hilary McD. *Centering Woman: Gender Discourses in Slave Society*. Kingston: Ian Randle Publishers, 1999.

Behrman, Carolyn. "'The Fairest of Them All': Gender Ethnicity and a Beauty Pageant in the Kingdom of Swaziland." Pp. 397–408 in *Dress and Ethnicity*, ed. Joanne B. Eicher. Oxford: Berg Publishers Limited, 1995.

Beller, Anne Scott. *Fat and Thin: A Natural History of Obesity*. New York: Farrar, Straus & Giroux, 1978.

"The Body of the Beholder." *Newsweek* 125, no. 17 (April 24, 1995): 66. Expanded Academic ASAP. Infotrac. University of Miami. Accessed January 7, 2004, <http://web3.infotrac.galegroup.com>.

Bogle, Donald. *Brown Sugar*. New York: Harmony Books, 1980.

Bordo, Susan. *Unbearable Weight: Feminism, Western Culture, and the Body*. Berkeley: University of California Press, 1993.

Boyle, Ed. "British Pounds-a-Plenty." *CBSnews.com*, March 26, 2004. CBS News. Accessed May 6, 2004, <http://cbsnews.com/stories/2004/03/26/uttm/main608783.shtml>.

Braidotti, Rosi. "Mothers, Monsters and Machines." Pp. 59–79 in *Writing on the Body: Female Embodiment and Feminist Theory*, eds. Katie Conboy, Nadia Medina, and Sarah Stanbury. New York: Columbia University Press, 1997.

Braziel, Jana Evans. "Sex and Fat Chics: Deterritorializing the Fat Female Body." Pp. 231–54 in *Bodies Out of Bounds: Fatness and Transgression*, eds. Jana Evans Braziel and Kathleen LeBesco. Berkeley: University of California Press, 2001.

Butler, Judith. *Bodies That Matter: On the Discursive Limits of "Sex."* New York: Routledge, 1993.

Carby, Hazel V. *Cultures in Babylon*. London: Verso, 1999.

Cargill, Morris. *Public Disturbances: A Collection of Writings 1986–1996*. Kingston: Mill Press Ltd., 1998.

Chancy, Myriam. "The Black Female Body as Popular Icon." Pp. 95–117 in *Essays on Transgressive Readings: Reading Over Lines*, ed. Georgia Johnston. Lewiston, N.Y.: Mellen, 1997.

Chernin, Kim. *The Obsession: Reflections on the Tyranny of Slenderness*. New York: Harper & Row, 1981.

Collins, Loretta. "'We Shall All Heal': Ma Kilman, The Obeah Woman, as Mother-Healer in Derek Walcott's *Omero*." *Literature and Medicine* 14, no. 1 (1995): 146–62.

Collins, Pat Lowery. *The Fattening Hut*. Boston: Houghton Mifflin, 2003.

Collins Patricia Hill. *Black Feminist Thought: Knowledge, Consciousness and the Politics of Empowerment*. New York: Routledge, Chapman & Hall, Inc., 1991.

———. *Black Sexual Politics: African Americans, Gender, and the New Racism*. New York: Routledge, 2004.

The Color Purple. Directed by Steven Spielberg. Starring Whoopi Goldberg and Oprah Winfrey. Warner Bros., 1985.

Condé, Mary. "Fat Women and Food." Pp. 124–31 in *Beyond the Pleasure Dome: Writing From the Romantics*, eds. Sue Vice, Matthew Campbell and Tim Armstrong. Sheffield, U.K.: Sheffield Academic Press, 1994.

Cooper, Carolyn. *Noises in the Blood: Orality, Gender, and the "Vulgar" Body of Jamaican Popular Culture*. Durham, N.C.: Duke University Press, 1995.

Crossing Delancey. Directed by Joan Micklin Silver. Warner Studios, 1988.

Cunningham, Brent. "Maya Angelou: Best-selling Poet Shares Story of Her Life and Work." *University of Buffalo Reporter*, April 30, 1998. Accessed April 17, 2003, <http://www.buffalo.edu/reporter/vol29/vol29n30/n3.html>.

Dangarembga, Tsitsi. *Nervous Conditions*. Seattle: Seal Press, 1989.

Dash, Michael. "In Search of the Lost Body: Redefining the Subject in Caribbean Literature." Pp. 332–35 in *The Postcolonial Studies Reader*, eds. Bill Ashcroft, Gareth Griffiths and Helen Tiffin. London: Routledge, 1995.

Deford, Frank. *There She Is: The Life and Times of Miss America*. New York: Penguin, 1971.

"Denise Belfon: Saucy Babe." Queenofsoca.com. Accessed June 14, 2004, <http://queenofsoca.com/ProfileDenise.html>.

Diop, Cheikh Anta. *Civilization or Barbarism: An Authentic Anthropology*. Trans. Yaa-Lengi Meema Ngemi. Brooklyn: Lawrence Hill Books, 1991.

Diprose, Rosalyn. *The Bodies of Women: Ethics Embodiment and Sexual Difference*. New York: Routledge, 1994.

Divas Live. Directed by Michael A. Simon. Starring Mariah Carey, Gloria Estefan, Shania Twain, Aretha Franklin, Celine Dion, and Carole King. Epic Music Video, 1998.

Easton, Alison. "The Body as History and 'Writing the Body': The Example of Grace Nichols." *Journal of Gender Studies* 3, no. 1 (March 1994). *Academic Search Elite*. EBSCO. University of Miami. Accessed September 12, 2003, <http://www.weblinks2.epnet.com>.

Edmondson, Belinda. "Public Spectacles: Caribbean Women and the Politics of Public Performance." *Small Axe* 1 (2003): 1–16.

Elliott, Missy. *This Is Not a Test*. Elektra, 2003.

———. *Under Construction*. Elektra, 2002.

———. *Supa Dupa Fly*. Elektra, 1997.

Ferguson, James. *The Story of the Caribbean People*. Kingston: Ian Randle Publishers, 1999.

"The Fifty Most Beautiful People in the World 2001—Jill Scott." *People Weekly* 55, no. 19 (May 14, 2000): 148. Expanded Academic ASAP. Infotrac. University of Miami. Accessed April 8, 2004, <http://web3.infotrac.galegroup.com>.

"The Fifty Most Beautiful People in the World 2003—Queen Latifah." *People Weekly* 59, no. 18 (May 12, 2003): 110. Expanded Academic ASAP. Infotrac. University of Miami. Accessed April 8, 2004, <http://web3.infotrac.galegroup.com>.

Franklin, Aretha. "I Never Loved a Man (The Way I Love You)." *Respect*. Wea, 2002.

———. "Respect." *Respect*. Wea, 2002.

———. "(You Make Me Feel Like a) Natural Woman." *Respect*. Wea, 2002.

———, and David Ritz. *Aretha: From These Roots*. New York: Villard Books, 1999.

Fraser, Laura. *Losing It: America's Obsession with Weight and the Industry That Feeds on It*. New York: Dutton Books, 1997.

Freeman, Carla. "Is Local: Global as Feminine: Masculine? Rethinking the Gender of Globalization." *Signs* 26, no. 4 (Summer 2001). Expanded Academic ASAP. Infotrac. University of Miami. Accessed January 7, 2004, <http://web3.infotrac.galegroup.com>.

Freud, Sigmund. *The Basic Writings of Sigmund Freud*. Ed. and trans. A. A. Brill. New York: Random House, 1938.

———. *The Interpretation of Dreams*. Trans. James Strachey. New York: Avon Books, 1965.

Frisch, Rose. *Female Fertility and the Body Fat Connection*. Chicago: University of Chicago Press, 2002.

Gatens, Moira. "Corporeal Representation in/and the Body Politic." Pp. 80–89 in *Writing on the Body: Female Embodiment and Feminist Theory*, eds. Katie Conboy, Nadia Medina, and Sarah Stanbury. New York: Columbia University Press, 1997.

Gilman, Sander L. "Black Bodies, White Bodies: Toward an Iconography of Female Sexuality in Late Nineteenth-Century Art, Medicine, and Literature." Pp. 223–61 in *"Race," Writing, and Difference*, ed. Henry Louis Gates Jr. Chicago: University of Chicago Press, 1986.

Glenn, Susan A. *Female Spectacle: The Theatrical Roots of Modern Feminism*. Cambridge, Mass.: Harvard University Press, 2000.

Goodison, Lorna. "Bella Makes Life." Pp. 75–84 in *Baby Mother and the King of Swords*. Essex, U.K.: Longman, 1990.

Gray, James, et al. "The Prevalence of Bulimia in a Black College Population." *International Journal of Eating Disorders* 7 (1988): 733–40.

Green, Kris. "Waterman to Quit 'Pop Idol.'" *Digital Spy* (March 16, 2004). Accessed June 26, 2004, <http://www.digitalspy.co.uk/article/ds13913.html>.

Gronhovd, Anne-Marie. "Writing the Woman-Subject: Marguerite Duras, From Theory to Fiction." Pp. 102–11 in *International Women's Writing: New Landscapes of Identity*, ed. Anne E. Brown and Marjanne Gooze. Westport, Conn.: Greenwood, 1995.

Hall, Stuart. "What Is This 'Black' in Black Popular Culture? (Rethinking Race)." *Social Justice* 20, nos. 1–2 (Spring–Summer 1993). Expanded Academic ASAP. Infotrac. University of Miami. Accessed March 28, 2004, <http://web3.infotrac.galegroup.com>.

Handler, Jerome. "Joseph Rachel and Rachael Pringle-Polgreen: Petty Entrepreneurs." Pp. 376–91 in *Struggle and Survival in Colonial America*, eds. David G. Sweet and Gary B. Nash. Berkeley: University of California Press, 1981.

Handy, W. C. *Father of the Blues: An Autobiography by W.C. Handy*. London: Sidgwick & Jackson, 1957.

Harrison, Daphne Duval. *Black Pearls: Blues Queens of the 1920s*. New Brunswick, N.J.: Rutgers University Press, 1988.

Harting, Heike. "The Profusion of Meanings and the Female Experience of Colonisation: Inscriptions of the Body as a Site of Difference in Tsitsi Dangarembga's *Nervous Conditions* and Margaret Atwood's *The Edible Woman*." Pp. 237–46 in *Fusion of Cultures*, eds. Peter Stummer and Christopher Balme. Amsterdam: Rodopi, 1996.

Hastings, E. A. *A Glimpse of the Tropics*. London: Sampson Low, Marston & Company, Ltd, 1900.

Hayes, Bob. "Ma Rainey's Review." *Chicago Defender*, February 13, 1926.

Heglar, Charles. "Named and Namelessness: Alice Walker's Pattern of Surnames in *The Color Purple*." *ANQ* 13, no. 1 (Winter 2000): 38. Expanded Academic ASAP. Infotrac. University of Miami. Accessed July 14, 2004, <http://web3.infotrac.galegroup.com>.

Hill, Errol. "On the Origin of the Term, Calypso." *Ethnomusicology* 11, no. 3 (1967): 359–67.

Hoffman, Melody K. "Hip-hop Innovator Missy Elliott: Reinvents Herself-Again-With New CD 'This Is Not a Test!'" *Jet* 105, no. 2 (Jan. 12, 2004): 58. Expanded Academic ASAP. Infotrac. University of Miami. Accessed April 8, 2004, <http://web3.infotrac.galegroup.com>.

Holden, Stephen. "Playful Aretha Franklin Plumbs Roots of Soul." *New York Times*, Nov. 5, 1994, late ed.: 15.

hooks, bell. *Black Looks: Race and Representation*. Boston: South End Press, 1992.

———. "Selling Hot Pussy: Representations of Black Female Sexuality in the Cultural Marketplace." Pp. 113–28 in *Writing on the Body: Female Embodiment and Feminist Theory*, eds. Katie Conboy, Nadia Medina, and Sarah Stanbury. New York: Columbia University Press, 1997.

"Houghton Mifflin Files Appeal Brief Arguing *The Wind Done Gone* Is Fair Use of *GWTW*." *Information About Suntrust v. Houghton Mifflin Company*. May 7, 2002. Houghton Mifflin. Accessed July 16, 2003, <http://houghtonmifflinbooks.com/features/randall_url/statement.shtml>. Path: "Houghton Mifflin Files Appeal."

Hsu, L. K. George. "Are the Eating Disorders Becoming More Common Among Blacks?" *International Journal of Eating Disorders* 7 (1988): 113–24.

Igor, Garine De, and Georgius J. A. Koppert. "Guru-Fattening Sessions among the Massa." *Ecology of Food and Nutrition* 25 (1991): 1–28.

"Julius and Ethel Rosenberg (Summary)." *Freedom of Information Act*. FBI. Accessed November 28, 2003, <http://foia.fbi.gov/roberg.htm>.

"Kate Smith Biography." Accessed May 6, 2004, <http://katesmith.org/katebio.html>.

Kent, Le'a. "Fighting Abjection: Representing Fat Women." Pp. 130–52 in *Bodies Out of Bounds: Fatness and Transgression*, eds. Jana Evans Braziel and Kathleen LeBesco. Berkeley: University of California Press, 2001.

Kerr, Paulette A. "Victims or Strategists? Female Lodging-house Keepers in Jamaica." Pp. 197–212 in *Engendering History: Caribbean Women in Historical*

Perspective, eds. Verene Shepherd, Bridget Brereton and Barbara Bailey. Kingston: Ian Randle Publishers, 1995.

Kessler, Joyce. "All the Horned Island's Birds: The Transformative African Symbols of Walcott's *Omeros*." *Arkansas Review* 5, nos. 1–2 (August 1996): 1–9.

Kiple, Kenneth F., and Virginia H. Kiple. "Deficiency Diseases in the Caribbean." Pp. 785–94 in *Caribbean Slavery in the Atlantic World*, eds. Verene Shepherd and Hilary McD. Beckles. Kingston: Ian Randle Publishers, 2000.

Knight, Franklin W. *The Caribbean: A Genesis of a Fragmented Nationalism*. Oxford: Oxford University Press, 1990.

Kramer, Heinrich, and James Sprenger. *The Malleus Maleficarum*. Trans. Montague Summers. New York: Dover Publications, 1971.

Lieb, Sandra R. *Mother of the Blues: A Study of Ma Rainey*. Amherst: University of Massachusetts Press, 1981.

The Life and Times of Sara Baartman the Hottentot Venus. Directed by Zola Maseko. First Run/Icarus Films, 1998.

Lorde, Audre. "Uses of the Erotic: The Erotic as Power." Pp. 53–59 in *Sister Outsider: Essay and Speeches by Audre Lorde*. Freedom, Calif.: Crossing Press, 1984.

———. *Zami: A New Spelling of My Name*. Freedom, Calif.: Crossing Press, 1982.

Lorenz, Paul H. "Anorexia and the Experience of Colonization in Tsitsi Dangarembga's *Nervous Conditions*." *The Philological Review* 23, no. 2 (1997): 41–51.

Magubane, Zine. "Which Bodies Matter? Feminism, Poststructuralism, Race, and the Curious Theoretical Odyssey of the 'Hottentot Venus.'" *Gender & Society: Official Publication of Sociologists of Women in Society* 15, no. 6 (2001): 816–34.

Mair, Lucille Mathurin. "Recollections of a Journey Into a Rebel Past." Pp. 51–60 in *Caribbean Women Writers: Essays From the First International Conference*, ed. Selwyn R. Cudjoe. Wellesley, Mass.: Calaloux Publications, 1990.

Mama Benz: An African Market Woman. Directed by Katia Forbert Petersen. Videocasette. SFINX Film/TV, 1993.

Marx, Karl. *Capital: A Critique of Political Economy*. Trans. Samuel Moore and Edward Aveling. Ed. Frederick Engels. New York: The Modern Library, 1906.

Minkler, Julie A. "Helen's Calibans: A Study of Gender Hierarchy in Derek Walcott's *Omeros*." *World Literature Today* 67, no. 2 (Spring 1993): 272–76.

Mintz, Sidney, and Douglas Hall. "The Origins of the Jamaican Internal Marketing System." Pp. 758–73 in *Caribbean Slavery in the Atlantic World*, eds. Verene Shepherd and Hilary McD. Beckles. Kingston: Ian Randle Publishers, 2000.

"Miss Piggy Goes Hog Wild for Denny's Restaurants." *Brandweek* (May 20, 2002): 5. Expanded Academic ASAP. Infotrac. University of Miami. Accessed November 3, 2003, <http://web3.infotrac.galegroup.com>.

"Miss Piggy Stars in Baked Lay's Ad." *The New York Times*, August 2, 1996: 22. Expanded Academic ASAP. Infotrac. University of Miami. Accessed November 3, 2003, <http://web3.infotrac.galegroup.com>.

Missy "Misdemeanor" Elliott: Hits of Miss E . . . The Videos. Starring Missy Elliott. Elektra, 2001.

Modleski, Tania, "Cinema and The Dark Continent: Race Gender in Popular Film." P. 221 in *Writing on the Body: Female Embodiment and Feminist Theory*, eds. Katie Conboy, Nadia Medina, and Sarah Stanbury. New York: Columbia University Press, 1997.

Monday's Girls. Directed by Ngozi Onwyrah. Videocassette. California Newsreel, 1994.

Morrison, Toni. *Beloved*. New York: Knopf, 1987.

Morton, Patricia. *Disfigured Images: The Historical Assault on Afro-American Women*. New York: Greenwood Press, 1991.

Narain, Denise deCaires. "The Body of the Woman in the Text: The Novels of Erna Brodber." Pp. 97–116 in *Caribbean Women Writers: Fictions in English*, eds. Mary Condé, and Thorunn Lonsdale. New York: St. Martin's Press, 1999.

Naylor, Gloria. *Mama Day*. New York: Vintage Contemporaries, 1993.

Neumann, Erich. *The Great Mother: An Analysis of the Archetype*. Bollingen Series 47. Princeton, N.J.: Princeton University Press, 1963.

Nichols, Grace. "The Battle with Language." Pp. 283–89 in *Caribbean Women Writers: Essays from the First International Conference*, ed. Selwyn R. Cudjoe. Wellesley, Mass.: Calaloux Publications, 1990.

———. *The Fat Black Woman's Poems*. London: Virago Press, 1984.

Norment, Lynn. "Queen Latifah's Roller-coaster Ride to the Top." *Ebony* 58, no. 6 (April 2003): 152. Expanded Academic ASAP. Infotrac. University of Miami. Accessed April 8, 2004, <http://web3.infotrac.galegroup.com>.

"Oh Sow Chic." *Time* (Nov. 2, 1998): 115. Expanded Academic ASAP. Infotrac. University of Miami. Accessed November 3, 2003, <http://web3.infotrac.galegroup.com>.

Okri, Ben. *The Famished Road*. New York: Anchor Books, 1993.

Olsen, Eric P. "Mountain Rebels: Nanny of the Maroons." *World and I* 15, no. 2 (Feb. 2000): 234.

"The Original Do-Right Woman: The Queen of Soul Talks about Her Life, Her Loves, Her Fear of Flying and the Time She and Sam Cooke 'Almost Went There.'" *Newsweek* (Oct. 4, 1999): 68.

"'The Parkers' Win Big Laughs as No. 1 Show in Black Households." *Jet* 10 (April 2000): 58. Expanded Academic ASAP. Infotrac. University of Miami. Accessed November 3, 2003, <http://web3.infotrac.galegroup.com>.

Patterson, H. Orlando. *The Children of Sisyphus*. Boston: Houghton Mifflin, 1965.

p'Bitek, Okot. *Song of Lawino and Song of Ocol*. London: Heinemann, 1984.

"The Problem." *Eating Disorder Information Network*. Accessed January 26, 2004, <http://www.edin-ga.org/about_us.asp>.

Pursell, Chris. "Monique Has Got Things To Say; 'Parkers' Star May Host '04 Talk Show." *Investment News* (March 24, 2003): 3. Expanded Academic ASAP. Infotrac. University of Miami. Accessed November 3, 2003, <http://web3.infotrac.galegroup.com>.

Queen Latifah. *All Hail the Queen*. Tommy Boy, 1989.

———. *The Internet Movie Database*. Accessed April 8, 2004, <http://www.imdb.com/name/nm0001451/>.

Randall, Alice. *The Wind Done Gone*. Boston: Houghton Mifflin, 2001.

Reed, Teresa. *The Holy Profane*. Lexington: University Press of Kentucky, 2003.

Richards, Meg. "Bill Gates Still Leads Billionaires' List." *Information Week* (March 1, 2003). Expanded Academic ASAP. Infotrac. University of Miami. Accessed April 8, 2004, <http://web3.infotrac.galegroup.com>.

Riis, Thomas. "Blacks on the Musical Stage." Pp. 29–50 in *Images of Blacks in American Culture*, ed. Jessie Carney Smith. New York: Greenwood Press, 1988.

Riley, Joan. *Romance*. London: Women's Press, 1988.

Riverol, A. R. *Live From Atlantic City*. Bowling Green, Ohio: Bowling Green State University Popular Press, 1992.

Roberts, Deborah. "A Whole New Her: After Dropping 150 Pounds, Carnie Wilson Is Taking on New Challenges." *ABCNews*. May 30, 2004. Accessed June 30, 2004, <http://www.abcnews.go.com/sections/2020/Entertainment/Wilson 030530_Carnie.html>.

Robertson, Glory. "Pictorial Sources for Nineteenth-Century Women's History: Dress as a Mirror of Attitudes to Women." Pp. 111–22 in *Engendering History: Caribbean Women in Historical Perspective*, eds. Verene Shepherd, Bridget Brereton and Barbara Bailey. Kingston: Ian Randle Publishers, 1995.

Robinson-Walcott, Kim. "Carnival Meets Dancehall: Winkler's Vision of Heaven in *The Duppy*." *Sargasso* 10 (2000): 25–37.

Rohlehr, Gordon. *Calypso and Society in Pre-independence Trinidad*. Port of Spain: Gordon Rohlehr, 1990.

Samuels, Allison. "Wall of Soul: Jill Scott Is Part of a Generation of 'Neo-Soul' Artists Who Are Reinventing a Classic Tradition while still 'Keeping It Real' for Black Audiences." *Newsweek* (April 9, 2000). Expanded Academic ASAP. Infotrac. University of Miami. Accessed April 8, 2004, <http://web3.infotrac .galegroup.com>.

Santelli, Robert. "A Century of the Blues." Pp. 12–59 in *Martin Scorsese Presents The Blues: A Musical Journey*, eds. Peter Guralnick et al. New York: Amistad, 2003.

Sayles, Genie Polo. How to Win Pageants. Texas: Wordware Publishing, 1990.

Scanlon, Mara. "The Divine Body in Grace Nichols's *The Fat Black Woman's Poems*." *World Literature Today: A Quarterly of the University of Oklahoma* 1 (Winter 1998): 59–66.

The Scarlet Letter. Directed by Roland Joffé. Hollywood Pictures, 1995.

Schindehette, Susan. "Kermit, Miss Piggy, Big Bird, Grover and Kids All Over the World Mourn the Loss of Muppetmeister Jim Henson." *People Weekly* (May 28, 1990): 119. Expanded Academic ASAP. Infotrac. University of Miami. Accessed 2003, <http://web3.infotrac.galegroup.com>.

Schneider, Dorothy, and Carl J. Schneider. *Slavery in America: From Colonial Times to the Civil War*. New York: Facts on File, 2000.

Seacole, Mary. *The Wonderful Adventures of Mrs. Seacole in Many Lands*. New York: Oxford University Press, 1988.

Sean Paul. "Punkie." *Dutty Rock*. Atlantic, 2003.

"Settlement Reached Regarding *The Wind Done Gone*." *Information About Suntrust v. Houghton Mifflin Company*. May 9, 2002. Houghton Mifflin. Accessed July 16, 2003, <http://houghtonmifflinbooks.com/features/randall_url/statement .shtml>. Path: "Settlement Reached."

"Sex and Body Image Survey." *Elle / MSNBC.com*. Accessed March 30, 2004, <http://www.elle.com/article.asp?section_id=14&article_id=2363&page_ number=1>.

Sheller, Mimi. *Consuming the Caribbean*. London: Routledge, 2003.

Sir Mix-a-Lot. "Baby Got Back." *Mack Daddy*. American, 2002.

Spiegler, Marc. "Marketing Street Culture: Bringing Hip-Hop Style to the Mainstream." *American Demographics* 18, no. 11 (Nov. 1996): 28–35. Expanded Academic ASAP. Infotrac. University of Miami. Accessed August 8, 2004, <http://web3.infotrac.galegroup.com>.

"Steatopygia." *Merriam-Webster's Online Dictionary*. 2004. University of Miami Ibisweb. Accessed July 6, 2004.

Steele, Cassie. "Remembering 'The Great Mother of Us All': Audre Lorde's Journey Through History to Herself." Pp. 77–88 in *Gendered Memories*. Amsterdam: Rodopi, 2000.

Stepan, Peter, ed. *Icons of Europe*. New York: Prestel, 2002.

Stolzoff, Norman C. *Wake the Town and Tell the People: Dancehall Culture in Jamaica*. Durham, N.C.: Duke University Press, 2000.

Stone, Angie. *Black Diamond*. Arista, 1999.

Storhoff, Gary. "'The Only Voice Is Your Own': Gloria Naylor's Revision of *The Tempest*." *African American Review* 29, no. 1 (Spring 1995): 35–45.

Stukator, Angela. "'It's Not Over Until The Fat Lady Sings': Comedy, and the Carnivalesque, and Body Politics." Pp. 197–213 in *Bodies Out of Bounds: Fatness and Transgression*, eds. Jana Evans Braziel and Kathleen LeBesco. Berkeley: University of California Press, 2001.

Summers, Montague. "Introduction to the 1948 Edition." Pp. v–x in *The Malleus Maleficarum*. By Heinrich Kramer and James Sprenger. Trans. Montague Summers. New York: Dover Publications, 1971.

Thompson, Robert Farris. *Flash of the Spirit: African and Afro-American Art and Philosophy*. New York: Vintage Books, 1984.

Toll, Robert C. *Blacking Up: The Minstrel Show in Nineteenth-Century America*. New York: Oxford University Press, 1974.

"Toni Morrison and Major Literary Associations Join Leading authors and Scholars in Opposition to Mitchell Trusts' Efforts to Prevent Book Publication." *Information About Suntrust v. Houghton Mifflin Company*. April 16, 2002. Houghton Mifflin. Accessed July 16, 2003, <http://houghtonmifflinbooks.com/features/randall_url/statement.shtml>. Path: "Toni Morrison."

Tucker, Lindsey. "Recovering the Conjure Woman: Texts and Contexts in Gloria Naylor's *Mama Day*." Pp. 143–58 in *The Critical Response to Gloria Naylor*, eds. Sharon Felton and Michelle C. Loris. Westport, Conn.: Greenwood Press, 1997.

Tucker, Sophie. *Some of These Days: The Autobiography of Sophie Tucker*. Garden City, N.Y.: Doubleday, Doran & Company, Inc., 1945.

Tuelon, Alan. "Nanny—Maroon Chieftainess." *Caribbean Quarterly* 19, no. 4 (1973): 2–27.

Ulysse, Gina. "Uptown Ladies and Downtown Women: Female Representations of Class and Color in Jamaica." *Ariel* (1999): 147–72.

———. "Uptown Ladies and Downtown Women: Informal Commercial Importing and the Social/Symbolic Politics of Identities in Jamaica." Ph.D. dissertation. University of Michigan, 1999.

"U.S. Consumer Debt Growth 'Alarming.'" *United Press International*, Jan. 13, 2004. Expanded Academic ASAP. Infotrac. University of Miami. Accessed July 17, 2004, <http://web3.infotrac.galegroup.com>.

Ustanny, Avia. "200 Years of Christmas." *Jamaica Gleaner Online* (15 Dec. 2001). Accessed Nov. 29, 2005, <http://www.jamaica gleaner.com/gleaner/20011215/life/life2.html>.

Van Sertima, Ivan. *Black Women in Antiquity*. New Brunswick, N.J.: Transaction Publishers, 1987.

Veit-Weld, Flora. "Borderlines of the Body in African Women's Writing." Pp. 123–34 in *Borderlands: Negotiating Boundaries in Postcolonial Writing*, ed. Monika Reif-Hulser. Amsterdam: Rodopi, 1999.

Vice, Sue. "The Well-Rounded Anorexic Text." Pp. 196–203 in *American Bodies: Cultural Histories of the Physique*, ed. Tim Armstrong. New York: New York University Press, 1996.

Visiting With Miss Lou. Videocassette. Creative Production and Training Center, 2003.

Walcott, Derek. *Omeros*. New York: Farrar, Straus & Giroux, 1990.

Walker, Alice. *The Color Purple*. New York: Pocket Books, 1985.

Welch, Pedro L. V. "'Unhappy and Afflicted Women?': Free Colored Women in Barbados 1780–1834." *Revista/Review Interamericana* (1999): 29. InterAmerican University of Puerto Rico. Accessed Jan. 30, 2004, <http://www.sg.inter.edu/revista-ciscla/volume29/welsh.html>.

Wiegman, Robyn. *American Anatomies*. Durham, N.C.: Duke University Press, 1996.

Williams, J. D., and W. J. Qualls. "Middle-class Black Consumers and the Intensity of Ethnic Identification." *Psychology and Marketing* 6 (1989): 263–86.

Willis, Deborah, and Carla Williams. *The Black Female Body: A Photographic History*. Philadelphia: Temple University Press, 2002.

"*The Wind Done Gone*: Questions and Answers About the Dispute." *Information About Suntrust v. Houghton Mifflin Company*. Houghton Mifflin. Accessed July 29, 2003. <http://houghtonmifflinbooks.com/features/randall_url/qandas.shtml>.

Winkler, Anthony C. *The Duppy*. Kingston: LMH Publishing Ltd., 1997.

Witcombe, Christopher L. C. E. "Women in Prehistory: The Venus of Willendorf Discovery." *Art History Resources on the Web*. Sweet Briar College. Accessed September 18, 2002, <http://witcombe.sbc.edu/willendorfdiscovery.html>.

———. "Women in Prehistory: The Venus of Willendorf—What's in a Name?" *Art History Resources on the Web*. Sweet Briar College. Accessed September 18, 2002, <http://witcombe.sbc.edu/willendorfdiscovery.html>.

Witt, Doris. *Black Hunger: Food and the Politics of U.S. Identity*. New York: Oxford University Press, 1999.

Wolf, Naomi. *The Beauty Myth: How Images of Beauty Are Used Against Women*. New York: Anchor Books, 1991.

Yarbrough, Martin. "Actress and Comedienne Mo'Nique of *The Parkers* Talks about Her Career, New Book *Skinny Women Are Evil*, New Fiance." *Jet* (Nov. 11, 2002): 58. Expanded Academic ASAP. Infotrac. University of Miami. Accessed November 3, 2003, <http://web3.infotrac.galegroup.com>.

Index

About the Author

Andrea Shaw is Assistant Director of the Division of Humanities and Assistant Professor of English at Nova Southeastern University in Ft. Lauderdale, Florida. She was born and raised in Kingston, Jamaica, and is a scholar of Caribbean and African Diaspora studies. She is also a creative writer and is working on her first novel. She graduated from the University of Miami with a Ph.D. in English literature, and she is now completing an M.F.A in creative writing at Florida International University.